THE KICKS SERIES, VOLUME 7

KRAV MAGA Kicks

בעיטות קרב מגע

Real-world Self Defense techniques from today's most effective Fighting System

Tested in battle: Kicking for no-nonsense self-preservation

By

Marc De Bremaeker

Fons Sapientiae Publishing

Krav Maga Kicks -Real-world Self Defense techniques from today's most effective Fighting System. Published in 2017 by *Fons Sapientiae Publishing*, Cambridge, United Kingdom

Please note that the publisher and author of this instructional book are NOT RESPONSIBLE in any manner whatsoever for any injury that may result from practicing the techniques and/or following the instructions given within. Physical and Martial Arts Training can be dangerous, -both to you and others-, if not practiced safely. If you are in doubt as how to proceed or whether your practice is safe, consult with an accredited coach, physical trainer, Krav Maga teacher or a trained Martial Art master before beginning. Since the physical activities described maybe too strenuous in nature for some readers, it is essential that a physician be consulted prior to any type of training.

Copyright © by Marc De Bremaeker

All rights reserved. No part of this publication may be reproduced or utilized in any form or by any means, electronic or mechanical, without prior written permission from the author and/or the publisher.
martialartkicks@gmail.com

ISBN of the printed version: 978-0-9957952-1-1

Recommended reading, by the same author:
"Isoplex - Musculation Program for an Aesthetic and truly Athletic Body (2017)
"Sacrifice Kicks - Advanced Martial Arts Kicks for Realistic Airborne Attacks (2016)
"Stealth Kicks - The Forgotten Art of Ghost Kicking" (2015)
"Ground Kicks-Advanced Martial Arts Kicks for Goundfighting" (2015)
"Stop Kicks-Jamming, Obstructing, Stopping, Impaling, Cutting and Preemptive Kicks" (2014)
"Low kicks-Advanced Martial Arts Kicks for Attacking the Lower Gates" (2013)
"Plyo-Flex-Plyometrics and Flexibility Training for Explosive Martial Arts Kicks" (2013)
"The Essential Book of Martial Arts Kicks" (2010) by Tuttle Publishing
"Les Coups de Pied d'Arret" (2017) in French
"Les Coups de Pied Bas" (2016) in French
"Le Grand Livre des Coups de Pied" (2016) by Budo Edition (In French)
"i Calci nelle Arti Marziali" (2015) by Edizioni Mediterranee (in Italian)

Dedication

*This book is dedicated with love to my third grandchild, but first granddaughter:
the beautiful
Abigail Wong Ze An De Bremaeker*

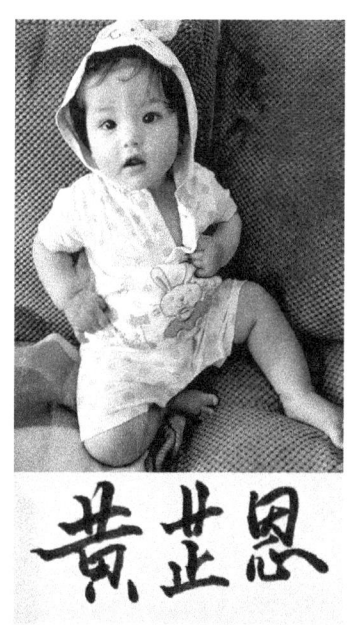

May G-d Bless and Protect Her.

**In every conceivable manner, the family is link to our past,
bridge to our future.
~Alex Haley**

Dear Reader,

In this day and age, the life of a serious author has become quite difficult. The proliferation of books and the explosion of internet content has made it nearly impossible to promote work based on extensive research and requiring complex lay-out.
Please enjoy this book. Once you are finished, I would ask kindly that you take a few short minutes to give your honest opinion. An unbiased Amazon review, of even a few words only, would be highly appreciated and encouraging.

Thank You,

Marc

Nothing is ever lost by courtesy. It is the cheapest of pleasures, costs nothing, and conveys much.
~Erastus Wiman

Acknowledgements

Without the active support of my wife and life companion, **Aviva Giveoni**, this book would not have come to life. Being an athlete in her own right, she understands the meaning of hard work and dedication.

Aviva

Sensei Shlomo Faige

Among many teachers and heads and shoulders above, my late Sensei, -*Sidney (Shlomo) Faige*-, should be mentioned with longing thankfulness. Sensei Faige founded the Shi-Heun style of Karate and Krav Maga.

Special Thanks to my life-long friend and training partner, **Roy Faige**, for his help and support. Roy is now heading the Shi Heun school is also my co-author of *The Essential Book of Martial Arts Kicks*. His influence and advice is felt in nearly every page of this work and the previous books in the series, where he appears in many photos.

Roy and Marc

Thank you to **Ziv Faige, Gil Faige, Shay Levy, Dotan De Bremaeker, Nimrod De Bremaeker and Itay Leibovitch** who helped by painstakingly posing for some of the photographs.

Most photographs have been taken by the author, by Roy Faige and by Aviva Giveoni. But special thanks have to be extended to talented **Grace Wong** for some shooting sessions. Thank you also to professional photographer **Guli Cohen**: some of the photographs in this book have been extracted from the photo sessions he gracefully did for previous volumes.

The drawings in this book are mine. Everything that I have learned about line art, I have done so from professional Illustrator **Shahar Navot**, who illustrated *The Essential Book of Martial Arts Kicks*. Thanks Shahar!

הבא להורגך השכם להורגו

"If someone comes to kill you, get up early to kill him first."
-Babylonian Talmud, Sanhedrin 72:1

Contents

Acknowledgements 7
Contents 8
Caution - Additional Dislaimer 10
Foreword to the 'Kicks' series 12
General Introduction 18
Introduction to Krav Maga 22

PART ONE   THE KICKS OF KRAV MAGA 25
1.   The Penetrating Front Kick 26
2.   The Upward Front Kick 30
3.   The Phantom Groin Kick 34
4.   The Low Front Kick 37
5.   The Pushing Front Stop Kick 41
6.   The Front Stomp Kick 44
7.   The Penetrating Side Kick 49
8.   The Pushing Side Stop Kick 52
9.   The Low Side Kick 54
10. The Stomping Side Kick 56
11. The Small Roundhouse Kick 61
12. The Bent-body Long Roundhouse Kick 65
13. The 'Low Kick' or Straight-leg Roundhouse 67
14. The Penetrating Back Kick 70
15. The Short Back Kick 73
16. The Upward Back Kicks 75
17. The Small Heel Back Hook Kick 78
18. The Crescent Kick 80
19. The Outside Crescent kick 81
20. The Outward Ghost Groin Kick 82

PART TWO   KRAV MAGA VULNERABLE POINTS TO TARGET..............85
Krav Maga's Vulnerable Points to Target..................87
   1. First Line Targets 88
   2. Second Line Targets 90
   3. Third Line Targets 94

PART THREE   APPLIED KRAV MAGA SERIES 101
   1. General 102
   2. Offensive Series 104
   3. Defenses against Punches 111
   4. Defenses against Kicks 124
   5. Defenses against Grabs 150
   6. Defenses against Holds 166
   7. Defenses against Chokes 183
   8. Defenses against an Armed Assailant ..196

AFTERWORD 206

CAUTION – Additional DISCLAIMER

<u>This special disclaimer comes in addition to, but not instead of, the general disclaimer presented on the first page of the book regarding the practice of Krav Maga and other physical activity.</u>

Most techniques presented in this book are crippling and potentially lethal. They are designed to be used in real self-defense situations where life and physical integrity are threatened.

The Author and the Publisher decline all legal responsibility for the possible consequences of using these techniques in training and in real life situations. The reader and practitioner is solely responsible for keeping an ethical behavior and for remaining in the legal framework for self-defense of the jurisdiction in which he is at the moment of use of said techniques.

Utmost caution and restraint are required both in training and in a real aggression. Krav Maga techniques have been designed for survival in extreme situations and common sense is required by the trainee.

All this having been said, the Author thinks that life is sacred, starting with yours and that of your loved ones. All normative citizens, because of their observance of social graces, are often reacting too slowly to obvious aggressions by criminals. Common Sense should always trump political correctness, although with caution. But honest folks should remember that, in extreme circumstances, it is *"Better to be judged by Twelve than carried by Six"*.

Foreword to the "Kicks" Series

A goal is not always meant to be reached, it often serves simply as something to aim at.
~Bruce Lee

The 'Foreword' and 'General Introduction' are very similar to those of the previous book in the 'Kicks' series. In order to spare a near re-read to our faithful readers of 'Low Kicks', 'Stop Kicks', 'Ground Kicks', 'Stealth Kicks' and 'Sacrifice Kicks' we invite you to go directly to the 'Introduction to Krav Maga' on page 22.

My Martial Arts career started with Judo at age 6. Judo was pretty new Fifty years ago, and a bit mystical in the Western World. A mysterious Oriental Art teaching how to use one's opponent's strength against him was a pretty attractive proposition for a wimpy kid. And the decorum and costume trappings made it a unique selling proposition. That is, until the Kung Fu craze of the Seventies, starring Bruce Lee, and then others.
In my opinion, what fascinated the Western masses, and the teen-ager I was then, was mostly the fantastic kicking maneuvers in the spectacular fights of those Kung-Fu movies. The bulk of the fight scenes were based on spectacular exchanges, the likes of which we had never seen before. What was new and revolutionary back then, may seem banal and common to today's younger reader. But we had been raised in the era of boxing and we had been conditioned by the fair-play of *Queensburry's* rules: we had no idea one could fight *like that*!
It was also the first time that the general public in Europe and America had seen a well-rounded Martial Art in action: punching, but also striking, kicking, throwing down, grappling, locking... It comprised all fighting disciplines in seamless aggregation. Wow! Judo was great, but I now wanted to *kick* like Bruce Lee. I therefore took up *Shotokan Karate*. 'Shotokan-ryu' is not the most impressive kicking style, but it was then the most developed Kicking Art outside of Asia and the only one available to me. It is as well and I certainly do not regret it. Though it is not an art known for extravagant kicks, Shotokan is very well organized didactically. It also emphasizes tradition, hard training, focus (*Zanshin*) and mastery of basic work. In all athletic endeavors, the continuous drilling of basic work at all levels of proficiency is the only real secret to success.

...And traditional Shotokan Karate drills and low training stances definitely fit this bill. So, during the whole of my career, I kept practicing Shotokan Karate, or a Shotokan-derived style at all times. I also kept at Judo, my first love. But in parallel, I started to explore other Arts a few years at the time, as opportunities and geography allowed. During my long Martial Arts career, I also did practice assiduously Karatedo from the *Kyokushinkai*, *Shotokai*, *Wadoryu* and *Sankukai* schools. I also trained for long stints of *TaeKwonDo*, *Muay Thai (in Thailand)*, *Krav Maga (in Israel)*, *Capoeira*, *Savate-Boxe Française*, two styles of traditional *Ju-Jitsu* and some soft styles of *Kung Fu*. This search is where I developed my individual methods and my own understanding of the Art of Kicking and its place in complex fighting. It also provided the basis on which to build my own personal research. Of course, this is strongly accented towards the type of maneuvers and training that favor my personal physiology and personality, but I have tried very hard to keep an open mind, among others through coaching.

Sometimes during this maybe too eclectic career, my travels took me to the **Shi-Heun** School of the late *Sensei Sidney Faige*, mentioned in the Acknowledgements. The *Shi-Heun* style is *Shotokan*-derived and mixed with *Judo* practice. It emphasizes extreme conditioning, total fighting under several realistic rules sets and the personal quest for what works best for oneself. And its self-defense training is based on no-nonsense **Krav Maga**. As this was only the early Eighties, this was definitely a prophetic ancestor of today's phenomena of Mixed Martial Arts of 'UFC' fame. The free-fighting rules in the *Dojo* were 'all-out' and 'to-the-ground', but this did not hinder the success of the School's students in more traditional tournaments under milder rules. The direct disciples of *Sensei Faige* did indeed roam the tournament scene undefeated for years.

Sensei Sidney Faige in action

In these days, points tournament fighting was mainly WUKO (World Union of Karate Organizations), with some notable exceptions like *Kyokushinkai* and *Semi-contact Karate* bouts. Unfortunately, WUKO generally (boringly) consisted in two competitors safely jumping up-and-down and waiting for the other to initiate a move, in order to stop-reverse-punch him to the body.

Sensei Faige with the winning Israeli National Team; the author and Roy Faige are on the right

When my name was called up in these events, there was usually some spontaneous applause from the spectators; they knew they were going to see, finally, some kicking. I apologize if it sounds like boasting; the point I am trying to make is that Karate fans of these times came to see kicking and rich fighting moves, and not some unrealistic form of boxing. And this is not to denigrate *Karatedo*, but more to critisize the castrating effect of unintelligent rules sets.

Marc and Roy facing off at the finals of a 1987 Points Tournament

Marc, kicking in point tournament

...It is my strong belief that Kicking is what made the Oriental Martial arts so appealing. As I have already mentioned in articles and previous books, I do firmly argue that *kicking is more effective than punching.* This usually causes many to stand up, disagree and maybe want to *punch* me, pun intended. This is an old debate, still raging, and I respectfully ask to be allowed to complete the sentence. I strongly believe that kicking is more effective than punching, **but proficiency takes much more time and work.** When presented this way, I do hope that this opinion is more acceptable to most. Let me detail my position briefly.

Kicking is more efficient than punching:

1. Because of the longer range

2. Because the muscles of the leg are much bigger and powerful than those of the arms

3. Because kicking targets, unlike punching targets, go from head all the way down to toes

4. Because kicks are less expected and therefore more surprising than punches, especially at shorter ranges

One needs to drill kicks from very close ranges as well

I readily admit that the opponents of my position do have valid arguments. They will point out that kicks are inherently slower than punches and can be easily jammed because they start from longer ranges. They will also point out that kicking often opens the groin, while forgetting that so does punching usually as well. It is my experience that, - *after a lot of dedicated and intelligent work-,* many kicks can be *as swift as punches and can be delivered at all ranges and from all positions.*

FOREWORD TO THE 'KICKS' SERIES

...During all my training years, I invested a lot of time, personal drilling and original research into Kicking Arts from all over the world. I experimented with all training tips gathered and I endeavored to try all mastered new kick variations in actual free-fighting and competitive tournaments. Here is the place to note that this is *not* about a huge number of different techniques; it is about finding the best possible techniques suited to one's specific strength, physiology and affinities (Once you have found your **few** techniques and the best way to drill them, then you focus on a fast and perfect execution from all ranges and positions). During my quest in the realm of kicking, I slowly developed a personal kicking style based on my personal history and mindset. I researched most of the available literature, but very few treatises were actually *dedicated* to kicking. The few works I found about kicking were generally very good, but usually style-restricted and unorganized. I never found the kind of book that I would have liked to have at the start of my Martial arts career. And so I decided to write it myself and share my global view of the subject. To the best of my knowledge, there has never been an attempt to compile and organize all the different Kick types and variation in such a way that it could serve as a reference work and the basis for exploration for the kick-lover. I did try to start this potentially huge work, probably imperfectly, with a series of Books I chose to name the 'Kicks Series'. A global overview of Basic Kicks was presented in **'The Essential Book of Martial Arts Kicks'** (Tuttle), translated in several foreign languages. Its success lead me to follow with the important lower gates attacks in **'Low Kicks'**, and then **'Stop Kicks'** about preempting, jamming, impaling, obstructing and 'cutting' Kicks. As a sign of these MMA times, the series was naturally enriched by **'Ground Kicks'**. **'Stealth Kicks'** then endeavored to cover misdirection and dissimulation while kicking. **'Sacrifice Kicks'** dealt with Jumping and 'Suicide' Kicks. And we hope that all this work will be built upon by others in the future. Now comes 'Krav Maga Kicks' with its focus on real world self-defense. As mentioned and underlined many times, kicking proficiency requires a lot of serious drilling. I have therefore also published a work about the basic general drills that will help you reach higher levels of proficiency. As in all athletic endeavors, it is the basic drills that will build the strong foundation needed; and it is to those basic drills that the truly good athlete will come back for further progress again and again. **'Plyo-Flex Training for Explosive Martial Arts Kicks and Other Performance Sports'** does present those general, basic but so-important exercises that one should regularly practice for continuous improvement of kicking proficiency.

And now last, but certainly not least: it is important to underline that my strong views do not try in any way or form to denigrate the Punching Arts. My personal philosophy is that Martial arts are a whole with a world of possible emphasis. A complete Martial artist should be proficient in punching, kicking, moving, throwing, grappling, evading and more. But every Artist will have his own preferences and particular skills in his own way to look at the Martial Arts as a whole.

...And here must I add the obvious: *there is no kicking mastery* without punching proficiency! Even for a dedicated kicker, punching (and striking in other ways with the upper limbs) will be needed for closing the gap, feinting, setting up a kick, following it up and much more... This will be made abundantly clear from most of the applications presented in this volume, just as it is clear from all my previous work.

It must be said that 'Punching' is sometimes the best or the only answer in some situations. I have known and met some extraordinary Punching Artists using kicks only as feints or set-ups. On the other hand, great kickers like legendary *Bill 'Superfoot' Wallace* were extremely skilled punchers and working hard at it, as I personally experienced in a few seminars. Kick and Punch, Punch and Kick: well-rounded is the secret.

And this leads me naturally to my last point. I would not want my books and my views to be misunderstood as an appeal to always kick when fighting, and especially not as an appeal to always high-kick. The best kicker in the world should not execute a high Kick, *just because he can*. A Kick should only be delivered *because and when it is suitable* to a specific situation! Obvious maybe, but certainly worth reminding. In someone else's words:

Take things as they are. Punch when you have to punch. Kick when you have to kick.
~Bruce Lee

General Introduction: The 'Kicks' Series

This series is not "How to" books for the beginner, but more, hopefully, a reference work for the experienced Martial Artist. It presupposes the knowledge of stances, footwork, and concepts of centerline, guards, distance, evasions and more. It also expects from the reader a good technical level in his chosen Martial style, including kicking. As this work is building upon the *Essential* basic level towards more sophisticated kicking maneuvers, all *Essential Kicks* are considered mastered from the author's point of view. The reader is invited to consult previous work already mentioned above. This book is intended as a tool for self-exploration and research about kicking outside experienced Artists' specific style. Therefore, the description of the different kicks is very short and typical examples are only briefly explained. The author relies more on photos and illustrations to exemplify his point. Let the reader try it and adapt it to his liking and morphology.

The author tends to prefer drawings over photographs to be able to underline salient points sometimes hidden in photos.

The experienced trainee will probably notice quickly that the basic background of the author is Japanese *Karate*. This cannot be avoided but was not deliberate. These books aspire to be as "style-less" as possible, as their purpose is to bridge across the different schools on the basis of common immutable principles. The author's philosophy is that Martial Arts are an interconnected whole, where styles are just interpretations of some principles and their adaptation to certain sets of strategies, rules, cultural constraints, or morphologies. It is one and same thing, although it may seem different from different angles. In the pictures and illustrations, the reader can see technical differences and adaptations from different styles. This is done on purpose to underscore the style-less philosophy of the treatise. Sometimes the foot of the standing leg is flat on the floor, as required in traditional Japanese styles, and sometimes the heel is up as in certain deliveries of Korean arts. It should be clear that the biomechanical principles are identical for trained artists and the small differences of emphasis are meaningless. It is more important for a trainee to adapt the technique to his morphology and preferences, once it is well mastered. This book series definitely does not pretend to present an axiomatic way to kick! In the same vein, arms during kicking are sometimes close to the body in hermetic guard and sometimes loose and counterbalancing the kicking move. Hands can be open, or fists tight.

...In the books of the 'Kicks' series, it has proved very difficult to name and organize the kicks into and within groups. The author has given the techniques descriptive names in English, whenever possible commonly used names. But the more complex, exotic and hybrid kicks have sometimes either several different appellations in use or none, while being difficult to describe. The names the author has chosen could certainly be disputed and improved upon by some. For the most basic kicks common to all styles, we have added the respective original foreign names. The author apologizes in advance to the purists of all styles: It is clear that the description of a technique cannot be in all details valid for all styles (For example, the basic Front Kick is taught differently in *Shotokan* karate than in *TaeKwonDo*). The original foreign names in Japanese, Korean, Chinese or Portuguese are just there as an indication for further research by the reader. It should also be noted that some techniques have different names in different schools of the same Art! For the more complex or exotic kicks, we have purposely omitted original names. Only when a kick is especially typical of a certain style, did we mention it, as a tribute to the specific school. The author also apologizes for his arbitrary transcription of foreign names, as purists could dispute the way it was done.

The kicks presented in this volume could be tagged "Advanced". This does not necessarily mean that they are more difficult to execute than the *Essential* basic kicks. On the contrary. Besides being a requisite of some form of classification, it mainly means that the principles behind the "basic" kicks should be first thoroughly mastered. A *Front Stop Kick* is relatively easy to perform and slightly different than a regular Front Kick. But for maximum power, it is important to follow the same principles of a basic Front Kick, with chambering, kicking through and chamber back. And the principles of the leg development stay the same for the more difficult Flying Front Kick. And even if a Low Front kick seems easy to perform, it will be done so under the same principles already mastered for maximum speed and power. A typical Feint Kick, the Roundhouse-chambered Front Kick is slightly tricky to master, but it is more a question of hip flexibility and acquaintance drilling: the principles behind the power of what is ultimately a Front Kick stay the same. Once the principles behind the basic Front Kick are mastered, all other "Advanced" kicks will be faster and more powerful. **This is all about mastering the basics and principles first**, and only later trying out variations in all kinds of situations, fancier or not. This is, by the way, true for any other physical activity. But because Advanced Kicks are more a variation on the theme of their underlying basic kicks, they will be presented in all their complexity by many variations in specific applications.
This volume will detail the *Essential* basic kicks relevant to Krav Maga...

This volume deals with practical Self-defense kicks only, as a variation of all six basic categories of Essential Kicks presented in previous work (Front, Side, Back, Roundhouse, Hook and Crescent Kicks).

Some Advanced Self-defense Kicks have been omitted, as the author felt he had to draw the line somewhere. Again the decision was arbitrary, and could be considered as open for discussion. First have been omitted the whole range of nuances of a given kicks: As already mentioned, the same basic kicks are delivered in slightly different ways in all different styles and schools. The small differences come from the different emphasis of each style, and do not alter the basic principles. The author therefore described the kicks in the way his own experience dictates as best, and each reader can adapt it to his own personality. Many possible variations are presented for completeness in the applications though.

Secondly, hybrid kicks variations have been omitted, as the infinite number of intermediate possible deliveries in between two kicks would make this endeavor ridiculous. For example, many possible kicks as hybrids of Front and Roundhouse Kicks exist, each one with different levels of emphasis on the "front" side and the "roundhouse" side. In this specific book about Jumping Kicks of all types, it is even truer: there are a great number of deliveries possibilities to execute a Flying Front Kick, as the length and height of the jump is highly dependent on the circumstances and the reaction of the opponent.

Unlike with the other volumes of the 'Kicks' series, this book will definitely consider Knee strikes as Kicks. Their importance will very quickly become clear to the reader.

Flying Knee Strike

The presentation of the Kicks suitable for Krav Maga will also be completely different from the general lay-out of the other books of the series. The relevant Kicks will be presented one by one, with a few relevant applications. The reader will then meet them again in the part of the work dealing with Defenses against common attacks.

Between both parts of the book, we shall also present the Vulnerable targets that the Krav Maga Artist must aim for in a confrontation.

The Self-defense series presented will be based on the important basic Principles of Krav Maga. Most importantly, they will generally include Kicks, among an uninterrupted series of Strikes, generally alternating heights and angles. Krav Maga is about overwhelming the opponent's senses and about seamless contimuous offensive action.

And now the reader is asked to remember that the fact that this particular book (and the whole 'Kicks' Series) has cataloged a great number of kicks does not mean that he has to know and master them all. As already mentioned, a good Martial Artist must first master the basics of his chosen style by hard work on the *Essential* techniques. Only when he has done so, should he try advanced maneuvers and special techniques from other Arts. He should then drill new and unconventional techniques, and then try them in free fighting. A real Artist will then know how the choose only *a few* techniques that are suitable to his morphology, psychology and liking. These very few techniques will then have to be drilled for thousands and thousands of times until they become natural. During the fight, it the *body* that intuitively choses the best technique to be used. If you have to think about what to do, you have already lost! Practice makes perfect. Again, in other people'words:

I fear not the man who has practiced 10,000 kicks once, but I fear the man who has practiced one kick 10,000 times.
~ Bruce Lee

Train hard, fight easy
~Alexander Suvorov

So drill the Kicks and the Applications as presented. Then adapt them to your physiology and psychology. Keep drilling and try them in hard practice and in free-fighting. The follow-ups presented are indicative only and intended to make you think. Try them before replacing by your own.

And now, let us go to KRAV MAGA KICKS...

Introduction to Krav Maga

FOREWORD מבוא

Krav Maga (קרב מגע) is a Hebrew word meaning basically "Close Combat". 'Krav' means combat or battle, and 'Maga' means contact in the sense of very close. Until its world fame as an effective Martial Art, the word was interchangeable with its previous generally accepted denomination: *Kapap* (קפ״פ). Kapap is the Hebrew acronym for: Krav Panim el Panim (קרב פנים אל פנים), which translates as 'Face-to-face Combat'. Basically, it means the same thing: Close Combat.

Krav Maga and/or **Kapap** is a self-defense system developed for the **Israel Defense Forces** (צה״ל) that consists of techniques based on simplicity and gruesome efficacy, and drilled in very realistic training. It is renowned for its focus on real-world situations and its brutal counter-attacks. As a rule of thumb, it emphasizes fast threat neutralization, simultaneous blocking and countering and an always offensive mindset. *Krav Maga* used to be used mainly by the Israel Defense Forces' special units, but it started to trickle down to regular army units, then to law enforcement and intelligence organizations, and finally, in a toned-down version, to the general public in Israel, and more recently internationally.

HISTORY היסטוריה

Imre Lichtenfeld (aka *Imi Sde-Or*) was born in 1910 in Budapest, Hungary and grew up in Bratislava (Slovakia). Lichtenfeld grew up to become a gifted wrestler and boxer. When, in the mid-1930s, anti-Semitic riots began to threaten the Jews of Bratislava, he became a street fighter and organized and trained Jewish young men to defend their neighborhoods against the growing numbers of Nazi and anti-Semitic hooligans. Finally, Lichtenfeld had no choice but to escape from Europe with his family in 1940. Arrived in Palestine, he joined Israel's "Haganah" (הגנה), a pre-state Jewish paramilitary organization protecting Jewish refugees from Arab marauders and also fighting for the establishment of a homeland for the persecuted Jewish people…

... It is then and there that Lichtenfeld met the *Kapap* training system already in place to teach Jewish refugees physical education, stick fighting and the rudiments of an evolving self defense system. Names associated with *Kapap* in the 'Haganah' and its special forces (called *Palmach*) were, among others: Gershon Kopler, Yitzhak Sadeh and Maishel Horovitz. In 1944, Lichtenfeld began training fighters in his areas of expertise: physical fitness, swimming, wrestling, boxing and both armed and unarmed street fighting. In 1948, when the State of Israel and the IDF (Israel Defense Forces) was founded, he became Chief Instructor for Physical Fitness and Close Combat (*Krav Maga*). He served in the IDF for about 20 years, during which time he developed and refined his unique method of hand-to-hand combat, based upon scientific principles and battle experience. The Middle East is a 'tough neighbourhood', to paraphrase Chief of Staff Ehud Barak. It is therefore by necessity that the Martial Art of *Krav Maga* evolved into the most realistic for the 20th and 21st centuries.

Imi Lichtenfeld

The Art evolved through trial and error, and through cross-fertilization with the experience of numerous Jewish Martial Artists who came and immigrated to Israel in its formative years. These Artists and their students did all meet through the special units of the IDF and influenced one another for the betterment of Krav Maga. Among a few, one can name **Sidney Faiga** and **Dennis Hannover** who, in 1960, immigrated together from South Africa to settle in Moledet, Israel. *Sidney (Shlomo) Faiga* later founded the *Shi Heun School of Karate and Krav Maga*, and *Dennis Hannover* went on to found the *Hisardut* (Survival = הישרדות) Organization.

Dennis Hanover and Sidney Faiga

Sidney 'Shlomo' Faiga

The fights and growth of the young State of Israel were the fertile soil in which all these influences brought about the genesis of a new and fully practical Martial Art umbrella: **Krav Maga.**

INTRODUCTION TO KRAV MAGA

Basic Principles עקרונות בסיסיים

Although **Krav Maga** encourages civilian students to avoid confrontation, it promotes finishing a fight as quickly as possible if it becomes unavoidable. Attacks are always aimed at the most vulnerable parts of the body, and training promotes the deliberate causing severe injury. Drills provide maximum safety to students by the use of protective equipment and by emphasizing caution and power control. *Krav Maga* is about 'real world violence, which unfortunately is still too common. And the key principle behind it is **KISS** (Keep it simple, stupid!).

The other general basic principles of *Krav Mag*a are:

- ***Attacking preemptively*** or Counterattacking as early as possible. Take the initiative as soon as possible.
- ***Keeping an offensive attitude***. Project confidence and proficiency. Avoid retreating and keep the pressure *forward*.
- ***Targeting attacks to the body's most vulnerable points*** (eyes, neck, throat, nose, ears, solar plexus, groin, lower ribs, knee, foot, fingers,...).
- ***Maximizing efficiency*** for fast neutralization.
- ***Using an offensive Defense***: simultaneous attacking and blocking
- ***Maintaining constant awareness of the battlefield*** (assailant's accomplices, surroundings, escape routes, weapons or useful everyday objects)
- ***Retzev*** (רֶצֶף). This probably the most important tenet of Krav Maga. *Retzev* in Hebrew simply means: sequence or continuity. But the connotation of the word in modern Hebrew is very much about un-interruption, smooth continuity, no stopping in a sequence of different steps until finished. American Krav Maga has it translated as 'Continuous Motion', which is a fair image. The idea of 'Retzev' is pretty simple: after your first offensive move [preemptive attack/attack/offensive defense/counterattack] you keep striking with no interruption until the fight is over: no resting, no interruptions, no retreating for assessment. And ideally, you should vary the type of attacks (punches/strikes/kicks), the height of attacks (low/high/medium), and the angle of attacks (inside/outside/back) in order to better overwhelm the opponent. Just do not make the mistake of assuming that this is about speed first; it is not! It is about continuity and full-powered intelligent strikes. Speed is good if it does not impact the focused power of the chain of strikes. Applications in the text will make the concept clear.

Part One

The Kicks of Krav Maga

הבעיטות של קרב מגע

The Kicks of Krav Mag*a* will be simple to execute in order to utilize the body natural reflexes to their maximum. They will never be 'High Kicks', so as to remain safe and stable, and as to keep the groin protected. They will target vulnerable points only. That's it!

Again **KISS**! Keep It Simple, Stupid.

1. THE PENETRATING FRONT KICK

The basic *Penetrating Front Kick* (See 'The Essential Book of Martial Arts Kicks') is probably one of the easiest Kicks to learn and execute, but it still needs assiduous practice. It is an aggressive forward maneuver, and therefore suited to the offensive spirit required. In *Krav Maga*, the Kick is used towards the solar plexus, the lower belly (below the belly button), the lower ribs (if the opponent is sideways or in a diagonal position) or the groin area just above the testicles (as the impact will both reverberate and will hurt the hip bones). If the opponent has his back to you, you can target the spine at kidneys level or the coccyx area (tailbone). *Make sure you train to target those points only*; visualize it when you hit the training bag, and concentrate on precision when drilling with a partner.
It is important to execute the Kick in its **Penetrating form**, and not in a 'pushy' way that dissipates power. An opponent hit by a good Kick stays in place to crumble... If your kick is a Pushing version, he will just be sent away.
The Penetrating form is illustrated with Drawings and Photos. Please note that only the rear-leg version relevant to basic Krav Maga; the front-leg variation is not powerful enough for optimum penetrating power by most trainees. As illustrated, lift the knee of your rear leg powerfully forward (at about waist level); this is the chambering position. Without interruption, you start extending the leg to develop the kick directly towards the target. Just before impact, you push forward with your hips. Penetrate the target by a few inches and pull your leg back towards the chambering position, from where it will be sent back to the ground rearwards (where it comes from) or forwards (both options must be drilled).

Penetrating Front kick landing back rearwards

If you are wearing shoes, the impact will be with the tip of your shoe. If you are bare footed, the impact will be preferably with the 'ball' of your foot (toes lifted as high as possible); you can also use the heel by flexing your foot, but it makes the kick a bit shorter and a little more 'pushy'.

Penetrating Front Kick landing forward

The hips push forward at impact for a penetrating kick

According to the principles of *Krav Maga*, it is best to land the kicking foot *forward* and to keep attacking the opponent aggressively; in order to end the confrontation as early as possible. In the illustrated example you take the initiative with an aggressive lunging (fake) Jab to catch his front hand. Pull on the hand while kicking his lower abdomen. Kick a few inches *into* the general groin area, and chamber back. Land forward while striking his nose with a direct Palm Strike (The fingers should aim at touching the eyes too).

Penetrating Front Kick to the groin area, with hand grab. Land forward to follow up with Palm Strike

The only Penetrating variations worth drilling for the Krav Maga Artist are both **<u>Oblique versions</u>** in which the opponent is not directly in front of you. You can need to kick obliquely to your outside (shorter) or to your in-side (longer). Your opponent could have moved to evade you, or it can even be about another attacker who needs to be dealt with. It is quite important to drill those variations on the heavy bag for familiarity. The coming Drawings and Photos will illustrate the technique and its importance.

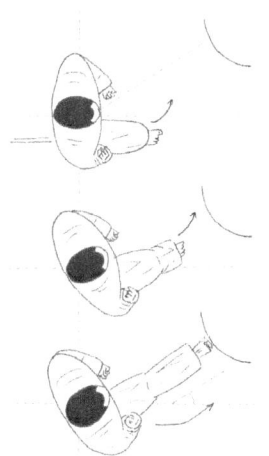
The Oblique Front Kick to the inside – top view

THE PENETRATING FRONT KICK

An Applied Oblique Front Kick

An applied Oblique Front Kick to your out-side: you look at the opponent in front, but kick the opponent on your side

Step diagonally out while punching, and execute a surprising Inside Oblique Front Kick to the ribs uncovered by the opponent's block

The technical execution of the Oblique Front Kick to the Outside

28   KRAV MAGA KICKS

Here follow two applications including a basic *Penetrating Front Kick*.
The Photos illustrate the stopping of an attacker's kick in its early stages: you execute the Penetrating Front Kick fast towards his hip joint or lower abdomen. Make sure it is not a 'push' but a '*kick-through*'. Take advantage of his being put off-balance and rattled by the shock wave in the general groin area: Catch his head by the hair or the ears, and pull it into a brutal Knee Strike. Aim for the nose, in order to blur his vision, restrict his respiration and cause demoralizing bleeding. Keep striking until the fight is clearly won.

The Illustrations show the use of the Penetrating Front Kick as a preemptive strike against a threatening assailant. Divert his attention up by throwing (brusquely and powerfully) your keys or anything else you have (dirt, book, wallet,...) towards his eyes. Kick towards his lower belly as he reacts up. And follow up with **Retzev**: Fingers to his eyes, Low Kick to the knee, Palm Strike to the chin or nose, catch his head preferably by the ears for a Knee Strike to the groin, Circular Elbow Strike to the side of the head (temple, ear, jaw hinge) or of the neck (carotid area). Do not stop until the assailant is fully vanquished.

Front Stop Kick to the hip of an kicking attacker, followed by Knee Strike to the face

Use an everyday object thrown towards his eyes to divert his attention up, kick towards his lower belly, and ... Retzev!

THE PENETRATING FRONT KICK

2. THE UPWARD FRONT KICK

The Upward Front Kick (See 'Low Kicks') is one of the important Kicks of *Krav Maga*, simply because it generally targets ...the testicles. In Krav Maga, there are no other worthwhile targets to be hit from below on a standing opponent: the chin and the armpit are great targets for a skilled practitioner, but too high to be considered by mainstream Krav Maga. Of course, if your opponent is bent over by pain or by a lock, his nose (face in general) will make a great target.

Upward Front Kick to the armpit: usually too high for mainstream Krav Maga

Upward Front Kick to the face of a bent-over opponent

The execution of the Kick starts, like for the Penetrating version, with a fast and powerful chambering of the rear knee. But this time, you will lift the knee just enough to allow for the development of the leg upwards all the way a few inches into the testicles. There is no need to lift the knee above what is necessary to achieve that. Moreover, the extension of the leg can start a little before the full chamber. There is no real hip push in this version;

The Upward front Kick to the groin

the only reason to push the hips would be to gain some range. Another difference with the previous Front Kick is the fact that this Upward Kick is more about speed than power: keep the muscles relaxed until impact in order to gain speed; the sensitivity of the target will make most of the work.

Connect with the top of the foot or the front ankle

The Illustrations show clearly the *difference of trajectory* between the Penetrating and the Upward Front Kicks. In order to maximize reverberating impact, the contact will be with the top of the extended foot, including the upper ankle (if you are close). It is vital to kick a few inches into target and not only slap it. Kick *through* a little, and then immediately pull the foot back into chambering position before landing. Not only is it not advised to let your leg linger around an opponent who could catch it, but the pull-back from the hit target confers some 'whipping effect' to the Kick that further increases the power of impact.

Upward and Penetrating Front Kicks start in the same way   *Hip Push and straight trajectory into the Penetrating version*   *No hip push and upward trajectory in the Upward version*

The Kick needs drilling on the **bottom** of the heavy bag (hanging at groin level of course), but remember that *speed* is of the essence.

This is a great self-defense Kick, and a few applied examples are presented here. It should be noted that the groin can be attacked in the same manner from the front *and from behind.*

Upward groin Front Kick after blocking a Front Kick

THE UPWARD FRONT KICK   31

Outside evasion against an Punching Attack, followed by groin Kick from behind

The two variations of the basic Kick with some relevance to Krav Maga would be the *Front-leg* version and the *Hopping* version.

The Front-leg version is trivial: it simply uses the front leg instead of the rear one, with the same chambering and development. Its importance resides in the fact that you should always be aware of your opponent's testicles and ready to hit them directly from the closest weapon. Sometimes, it simply means to lift the front foot up. The sensitivity of the target can excuse all sorts of short-cuts in terms of clean technique and power generation.

The front-leg Upward Front Kick

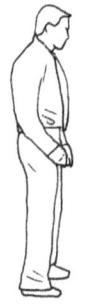   

Applied front-leg Upward Front kick: evade forward and in on a punching attack and lift you front leg directly into the assailant's groin

The Hopping version is also a front-leg version, but with more reach: your rear foot comes to take the place of your front foot (or even a little further). Your front foot is already on its way to the opponent's groin. *Everything happens fast in a low and subdued hop or a discreet Cross-step towards him.* It is imperative to avoid any telegraphing of the coming attack, like hand movements or a sudden bobbing up of the head.

The hopping Upward Front Kick

Hopping Front Kick can be a full hop...

...or can be a discreet cross step

An example of applied Upward Front Kick is presented below. Many more will appear in the text: this is a bread-and-butter *Krav Maga Kick*!

The ubiquitous Groin Kick: in this example after a preemptive high punch

THE UPWARD FRONT KICK   33

3. THE PHANTOM GROIN KICK

This is a great maneuver already presented in 'Stealth Kicks'. In the previous section, we have underlined the importance of being always aware of the placement of your opponent's testicles and of the shortest way to hit them at any time. This Kick is the embodiment of this concept: you are very close to the assailant and simply lift your foot into his groin, directly. In order to do that, if you are close, you need to open your knee to the outside and to connect with the inside part of the foot. This fantastic Kick can be delivered from the rear or the front foot.

The Phantom Groin Kick, Ouch!

The Phantom Groin Kick

After a punch in close combat

This is a fantastic Kick that you should drill a lot on the heavy bag or on the partner-hold striking pads. Drilling for speed and power is necessary to make this a supreme kicking maneuver. This Kick should be nearly automatic if you find yourself in this close range. It should launch without thinking!

A Kick worth drilling

Again, you must make sure that you **penetrate** the target for an inch or two, before you retract the leg; and then of course keep fighting (In the *Krav Maga* spirit of no stopping your offensive until the fight is over)...

... The Kick can be also used against the opponent's nose (face) if he is bent over for some reason or another. The following example, against an assailant rushing to grab you, shows the double use of the Kick: the groin first, then the face.

Groin-kicked opponent bends over to get phantom-kicked in the nose

A few more applied examples are presented below.

In the first example, you attack an opponent getting too close. As he bends over in groin pain, you strike the back of his neck (Hammer-fist or Forearm), you knee his face, and then hooking-uppercut-back kick his head as you move away.

Preemptive attack of close opponent

The reader is invited to remember that <u>**hi/low**</u> is usually the way to go; change of height of subsequent attacks will always overwhelm the opponent. Keep striking, of course.

High Jab, unexpected groin kick

THE PHANTOM GROIN KICK

This is obviously the kick of choice when you get grabbed from close up, for example in a Front Choke. Kick fast and use the paincaused to open the attacking arms. Use the momentum and the hips for a hand-blade chop to the side of the neck (carotid strike-through). This pulls a natural 'Low Kick', followed by an Elbow Strike. You can grab his head for a concluding Knee Strike to the groin (again).

Kick when caught in a choke, and start Retzev

The Kick is best used preemptively, but it can also be used as a Counter after blocking a punch. The attacker bends in pain into an Elbow Strike, and gets another Groin Kick. Then a Cross, then...

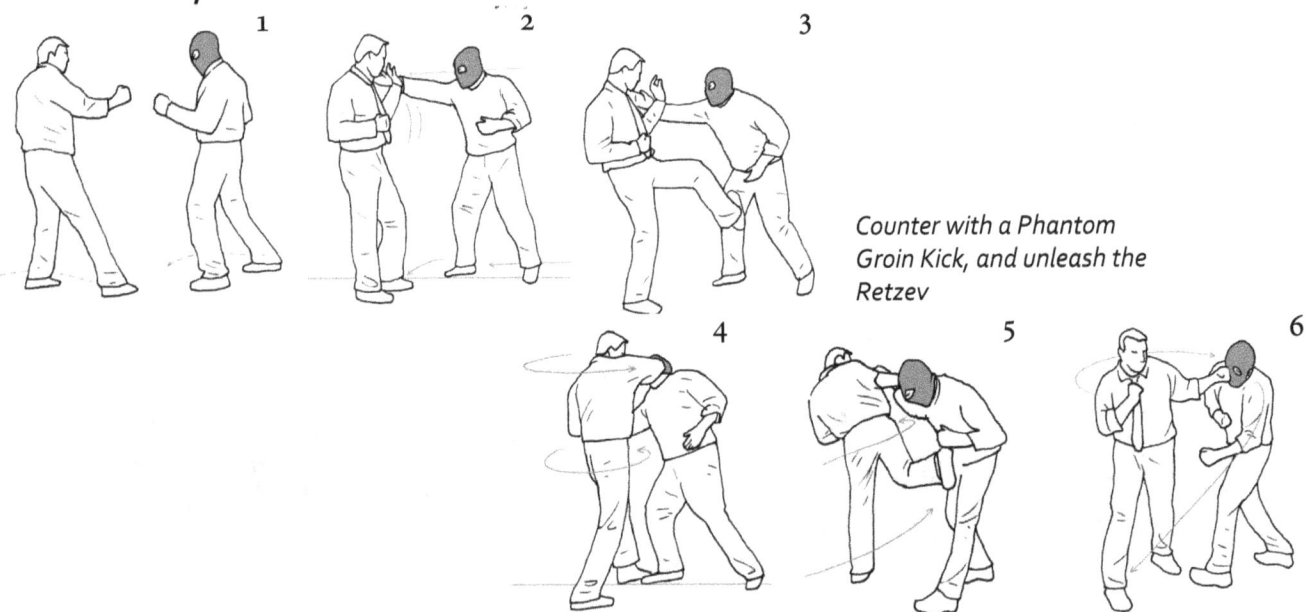

Counter with a Phantom Groin Kick, and unleash the Retzev

4. THE LOW FRONT KICK

The Low version of the Front Kick (See '*Low Kicks*') can be "Penetrating" or "Upward", or most of the time a hybrid between the two. In Krav Maga, the Kick targets the knee or the shin (from ankle, all the way up to knee). There is no need for a high chamber, but some chambering is required for power delivery: not higher than needed for leg development. Although the Kick seems simple and easy, it still requires training for a 'dry' and powerful automatic delivery. It is advised to

No need for a high chamber

Drill this Kick hard, it is worth your while

drill against an old tire in order to acquire the habit to kick powerfully an inch or two *into* the target. If you have drilled the Kick seriously in this way, it can be extremely painful at impact and you have a very surprising and debilitating weapon in your arsenal.

If you are wearing hard-soled (or –tipped) shoes, you will of course connect with the tip of the shoe (a few inches in!). If you are bare-footed, you can connect with the ball of the foot under the toes or with the in-side of the foot (soccer-style). Note that you can also deliver the Kick with some bending rearwards, to keep your head out of danger.

The Kick can be delivered straight or bending away

The soccer-style version

THE LOW FRONT KICK   37

An import aspect of good execution is maximum **Stealth**: you have to make sure you do not telegraph your delivery by moving your upper body in any way. Try to keep your lower body independent. You can even use your hands or voice for an idiotic and non-threatening diversion that will keep the opponent's attention up.

At the end of the section, we shall a few examples of applied Low Front Kick. This Kick is very under-appreciated. With some training, it becomes extremely fast, extremely easy to execute successfully, extremely painful and fantastic to start your winning combination that will end the fight. It can also be an annoying *Attrition Kick* that saps your opponent's will to fight, annoys him greatly and gets him expecting more of those just when you then launch another completely different attack. The Kick should also be nearly automatic when you get in range, and even more if you find yourself in a Clinch.

In a Clinch, immediately kick the shin and follow up with a Knee Strike

With the exception of kicking a downed opponent, the Kick should *exclusively target the shin* (full of nervous endings) on all its length, or the *knee* from all directions: the front, the in-side, the out-side and the back. But remember to always **kick through** for an inch or two. From the front, the ideal sensitive point would be just below the kneecap, in a slightly (natural) upward way.

A downed opponent can be kicked in the face or the ribs, and this should of course be followed by more attacks, until he yields..

Kick a downed opponent and follow up

There is a slightly more **stomping variation** of the Kick to attack the knee from above downwards. It is the *Tilted-heel version*, which requires a higher chamber and connects with the plant (bottom) of the foot. It also requires to kick through the target all the way (sometimes all the way to the ground). See at the top of next page.

KRAV MAGA KICKS

The tilted-heel, more crushing, version of the Low Front Kick

And here come a few applied examples, as promised.

A fast Low Kick to a **landing kicking leg**, or to a **stepping leg**, is very painful and will allow you to start a blitz *Retzev*. The same applies to the **standing leg** of a kicking assailant.

Kick the shin of a landing kicking leg

Kick the shin of a standing leg

Stop a Spin-back Kick by kicking the standing leg and follow up with a stomping kick into the back of his knee

THE LOW FRONT KICK

The Kick is great to stop the momentum of an attacker trying to rush you for a push or for a grab. Kick brutally *through* the shin of the stepping leg, let your leg come back to *rebound* on the floor and come back forward for a Groin Kick. You could follow up with a 'Low Kick', a Punch to the head, and a Knee Strike.

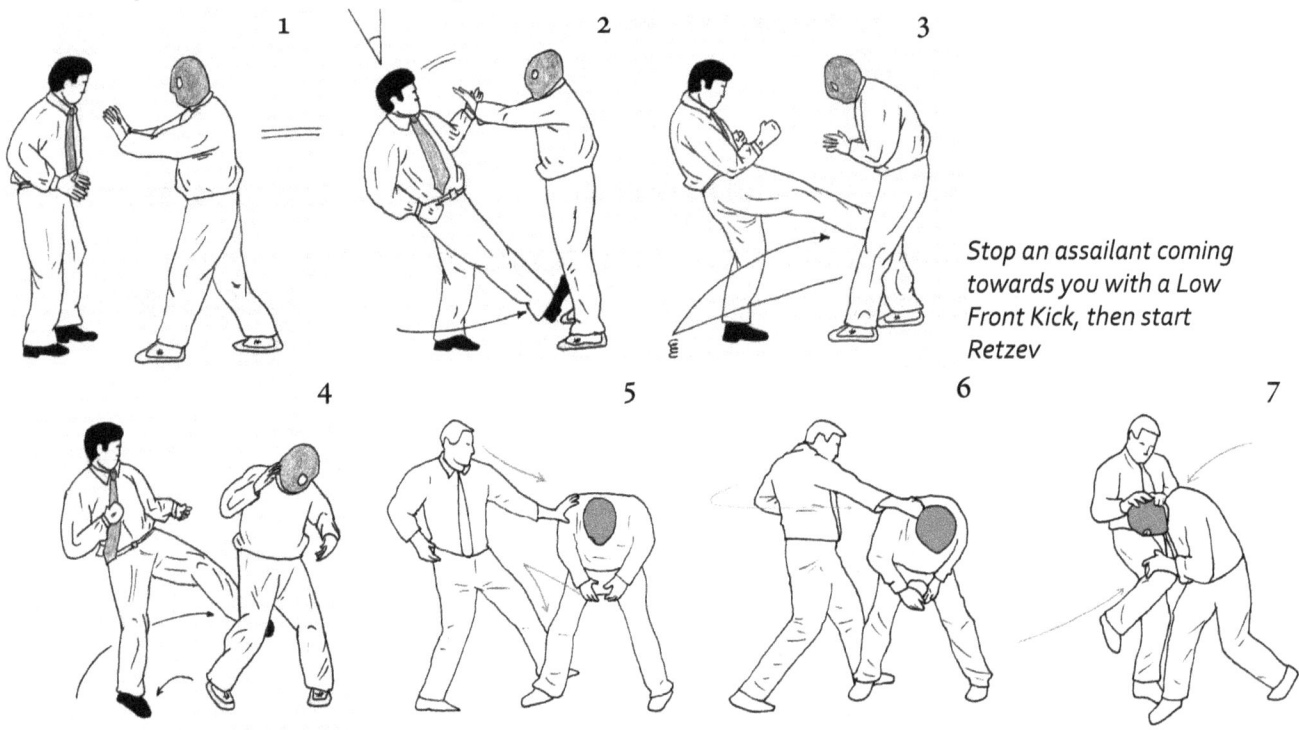

Stop an assailant coming towards you with a Low Front Kick, then start Retzev

And we shall conclude this section with an example of an **offensive** application. You attack your opponent with a high Jab/Cross combination towards the eyes. But your leg is also already on the way for a hard Low Front Kick. Follow up with another high Cross Punch to the face (aim for the nose), and then another Low Front Kick to the shin. Hi/Hi/Low/Hi/Low. And keep the *Retzev*...

Offensive Combination using the Low Front Kick

KRAV MAGA KICKS

5. The Pushing Front Stop Kick

This Kick is somewhat awry of the basic principles of *Krav Maga*. As its name indicates, it is a 'Pushing' Kick, and therefore not a decisive and potentially fight-ending technique as generally required from Krav Maga Principles. It is still an important maneuver to drill, because it is sometimes the only thing between you and defeat.

The Pushing Front Stop Kick

The Pushing Front Stop Kick is used to stop and repel the assailant. It is used when you have been surprised and need to stop an attacker to have time to gather your wits and start fighting. Once the attacker has been stopped and/or pushed away, you'll revert to the exclusive use of punishing techniques like the Groin Kick.

The Pushing Front Stop Kick

The Kick is in very common use in the hard Fighting Art of *Muay Thai* (where it is called '*Teep*'). This certainly proves its real world potential.

The Pushing Front Stop Kick: a Muay Thai favorite

The Muay Thai 'Teep' Kick – Aviva Giveoni

The Kick is a close parent of the Penetrating Front Kick, but the chambering is executed at mid-trajectory already, which gives the Kick its 'pushy' feel. See Application at the top of next page.

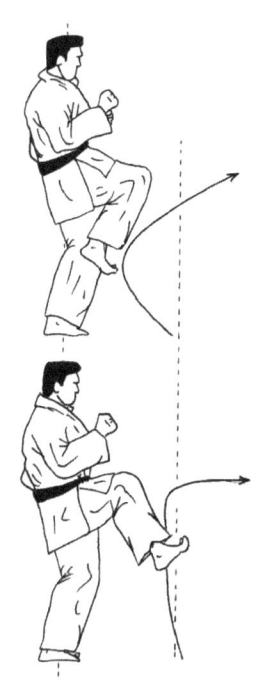

Comparative chambering of the regular Penetrating Front Kick and the Pushing Front Stop Kick

THE PUSHING FRONT STOP KICK

The Pushing Front Stop Kick, used against an attack by a Penetrating Front Kick

The Kick must be directed around the center of gravity of the opponent, from the solar plexus down to the lower abdomen, in order to be able to stop his forward momentum. If you have still time to finesse and focus, the ideal Krav Maga *Pushing Front Stop Kick* should be targeting the lower abdomen: in spite of being 'pushy', a strong impact to the lower abdomen will tend to reverberate to the testicles and rattle somewhat the opponent.

Try to stop-kick him in the general groin area

Remember though, that this Kick's aim is *to stop the opponent*; it should always be followed up by aggressive attacks: stick to your 'pushed' opponent and keep striking. If you have pushed your opponent far away, a good follow-up would be the *Hopping rear-leg Penetrating Front Kick*, sneaky in its unexpected range. A good example is presented at the top of next page. You stop-kick an assailant attacking you with a rear-leg Roundhouse Kick, aiming for the groin area. As your Pushing Kick has also sent him tumbling away, you follow with a Hopping rear-leg Penetrating Front Kick, also in the general lower abdomen area; this Kick is not 'pushy' but penetrating and chambered-back. Follow-up immediately with a Finger Strike towards the eyes, a 'Low Kick' through the front knee, and a Palm Strike to the chin (hi/lo/hi). You could then conclude with a hips-powered Circular Elbow Strike to the side of the head (temple/ear/jaw hinge), and a groin Knee Strike (hi/lo). Retzev is the key.

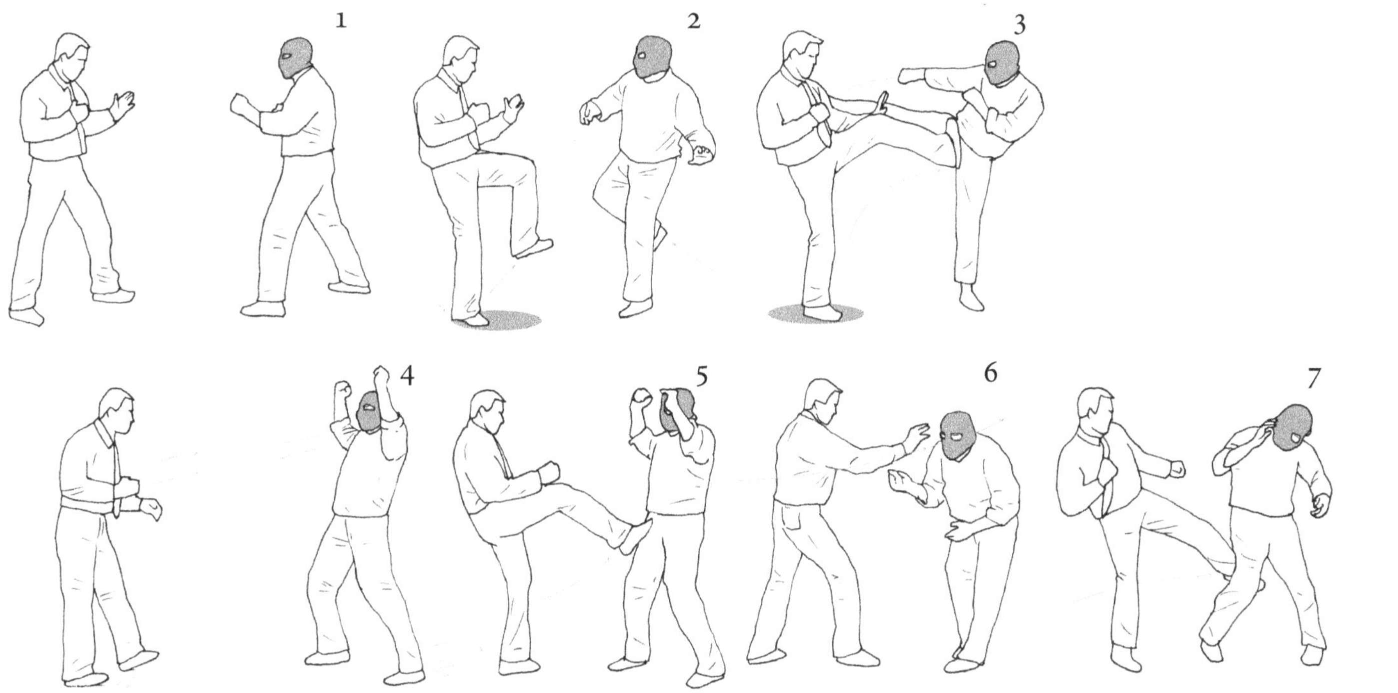

The Pushing Front Stop Kick followed by a Hopping Penetrating Front Kick to 'catch up' the pushed-away attacker

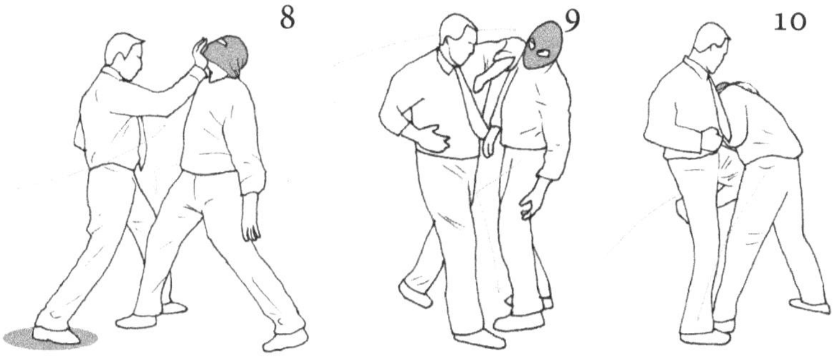

To conclude, it should be noted that the *Pushing Front Stop Kick* can also be used to stop an opponent's arm or leg travelling towards you. It is then more of a 'Leg Block' maneuver, but it can be useful as it can also cause damage to the joints of the attacker. It is still more of a defensive technique and, given the choice, Krav Maga would always go for the more offensive technique possible: if you can kick a chambering thigh, you can as well kick the groin a few inches away...

Stop Kick Block of an incoming Roundhouse Kick, and follow-up

THE PUSHING FRONT STOP KICK

6. THE FRONT STOMP KICK

The Stomp Kick may seem trivial, but it should be noted that it requires serious training to become the 'Judgement Day' technique it can be. A powerful Stomp to a sensitive target can simply conclude a fight, but the *Kravist* (Krav Maga Artist) must learn to kick with all his power (after some chambering) and through the target (as if totally crushing a bug). Intense drilling is needed on tires, bags, focus pads, ...

Chamber high and crush; simple but needs serious drilling

Crushing an opponent's ankle, toes, fingers, wrist or knee can definitely stop its aggressive intentions. Not mentioning the head, the lower ribs or the sternum of an opponent on the ground. Destroying a joint can make it physically impossible for an assailant to keep fighting when, sometimes, inflicting pain is not enough.

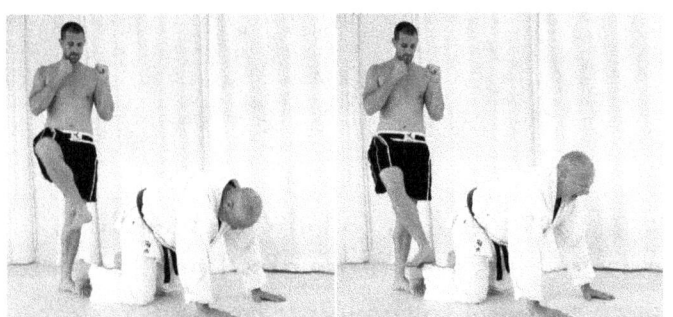
Stomping a downed attacker's Achilles' tendon will neutralize him with serious ankle damage; kick through and crush into the floor

Crushing an assailant's wrists or fingers will seriously hamper his ability to keep on

Stomp a downed opponent's lower ribs after using his legs to make him roll sideways; powerfully crushing lower ribs is an extremely dangerous technique

44 KRAV MAGA KICKS

Armpit/Ribs Stomp on an assailant downed after grabbing your lapel; you have struck his grabbing biceps and taken him down with an Outside Leg Rea

Aggressive release from a wrist grab ending in a rib Stomp; Palm Slap, Wrist Rotation, Chin Grab and Head Twist Takedown

The Stomp should be used automatically when in range: it is an extremely powerful, unexpected and disturbing technique. For example, it should be executed without even thinking about it if you suddenly find yourself in Clinching range. In that case, it could even be combined with a 'Soccer' Front Kick to the opponent's shin, followed by a scrape of same shin and a powerful Stomp of the ankle and upper foot. If, in that case, you keep your foot forcefully on his, simply pushing him back will cause him to fall and hurt his ankle joint. Such a combination, illustrated by the Photos below, takes drilling time to become automatic, but it is certainly worth the effort.

In a Clinch, automatically kick, scrape, stomp and push

THE FRONT STOMP KICK

The most practical Stomp Kick is the Front Stomp *with the foot generally pointing diagonally at 45 degrees*. It is mostly used to strike the back of the knee and stomp it all the way into the floor. It is ideal for use after deflecting a kicking attack.

The Knee Stomp from the front

Knee Stomp after kick deflection, when still in front of the opponent

Knee Stomp after kick deflection, when having gained the opponent's back; finish with a powerful Forearm Strike to the throat

When you 'have' the assailant's back, you can also stomp the back of the knee of his rear leg

46   **KRAV MAGA KICKS**

Two things must be remembered about the Stomp: Drill it and Use it!

For example, if you find yourself getting caught in a 'come-along' arm-lock, immediately stomp the back of the opponent's knee.

Stomp against an Arm-lock

The next Photos illustrate a Krav Maga release from the early setting-up of a standing Rear Choke: You have to react immediately and grab the choking arm. Then strike the attacker with a Buttocks Strike to the groin area and a Stomp on his foot. You can then make use of his pain to go into classic release that gets to his back in armlock position. Grab his hair to pull his head back and stomp the back of his knee.

Classic release from rear choke attempt, ending with a back-of-the-knee Stomp

The last Photo series, at the top of next page, illustrates the *Stomp* in a 'Retzev' follow-up, after blocking and redirecting an assailant's kick. Low Kick to the knee joint, Palm Strike and shoulder grab, and then Stomp to the back of the knee. The opponent is now totally at your mercy for further blows.

Stomp Kick after redirecting an attacker's Roundhouse and low-kicking the knee of the landing leg

בתחבולות תעשה לך מלחמה

"By way of deception, thou shalt do war."
~The Bible, Proverbs 24:6

7. THE PENETRATING SIDE KICK

The Penetrating Side Kick is one of the most powerful Martial Arts Kicks, because it maximizes the use of the hips and the lower back muscles. It requires training though, as the power comes from good technique and from the well-times pushing of the hips.

Body alignment position for good Side Kick technique

The technical Penetrating Side Kick

A powerful kick that requires good technique

Requires drilling, but a powerful kick indeed!

Krav Maga will normally use the **front-leg version**, generally with an aggressive forward hop. It keeps the fighter generally well protected during execution. The Kick will target the <u>hip joint, the lower abdomen and the lower floating ribs</u>. More experienced fighters will also target the armpit and the higher ribs, but it deviates from the 'no high kicks'-principle. The very best version is in fact presented separately further on, as **the Low version** targeting the knee.

THE PENETRATING SIDE KICK

...

*An applied offensive **front-leg** Penetrating Side Kick: note the cross step and the feint to cause the opponent to open his ribs*

Also targeting the hip joint or the upper thigh

Hopping into the front-leg Side Kick

This Kick is a great combination-opener. Its best version (excluding the Low Kick one to follow), is the attack of the *lower ribs* when the opponent 'offers' them by punching high.

Stop-kick the lower ribs as the opponent 'opens' them to punch

A very useful and practical version of the Penetrating Side Kick is the **<u>Body-bent</u>** one. By bending away, the fighter can keep his head and upper body away from any danger: like a Stop Punch, a high Kick or a weapon. This version has the advantage of not losing any power. It also helps both speed and power for the less flexible fighters who want to kick at ribs level.

➔

The Hand-on-floor front-leg Side Kick

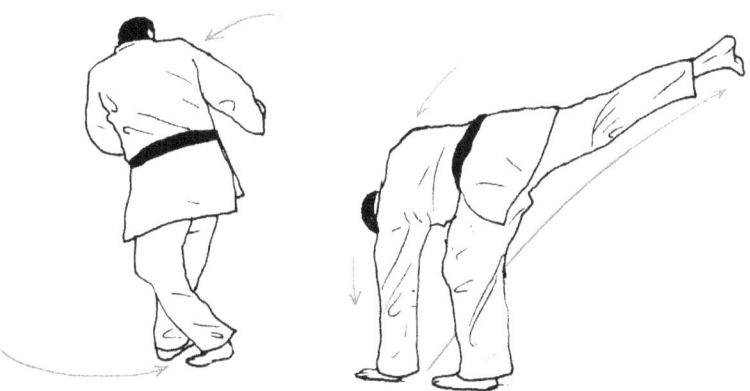

Three applied Body-bent Penetrating Side Kicks that keep your head away from the danger zone

To conclude this section, we shall present two applications against an overhead stick strike. (**1**) In the first (preferable) option, you stop-kick the ribs presented by the assailant as he arms his strike by lifting the stick up; you pre-empt the attack...
(**2**) In the second example, you are too late for a Stop Kick: evade the stick rearwards and outwards, and then come back in to kick the ribs presented by the momentum of the stick strike.

1

Preempt the attack by kicking as the assailant lifts his stick; follow-up with an Elbow Strike to the neck and a Knee Strike to the face, and...

2

Evade the downward stick strike and kick the ribs presented by the momentum of the missed attack

THE PENETRATING SIDE KICK

8. THE PUSHING SIDE STOP KICK

The 'Pushing' version of the Side Kick is also a great technique to stop an assailant and push him away, before you can retake the initiative. It is more powerful than the Pushing Front Stop Kick, and it should be preferred when possible. Just like for the Front Stop Kick, the *Pushing Side Stop Kick* gets into chambering position further on its trajectory, in order to save time and keep the foot between you and the attacker; this is illustrated by the comparative Drawing.

Comparison of Chambering position of the regular Penetrating Side Kick and the Stop Pushing Side Kick

In order to stop a forward momentum, it will have to target *the ribs, the solar plexus, the hip joint or the lower abdomen*. Its best stopping version though, will be the Low version targeting the front knee of the attacker. The ideal 'high' version of the kick should target the lower ribs of a punching attacker who does not protect them. But the technique is also excellent at stopping kicking attacks in their tracks.

Pushing Side Stop Kick to the ribs

Pushing Side Stop kick to the knee

Stopping a kicking attack and pushing the assailant away

KRAV MAGA KICKS

The Body-bent variation of the Side Kick is relevant to the Pushing Stop version too:

The Body-bent version of the Pushing Stop Kick has the advantage of keeping your head away from danger

Once you have stopped and/or pushed back your attacker, remember that you should aggressively pursue him in order to prevent him from taking back the initiative. Remember: **Retzev**!

1

Preempt the opponent's step or attack, strike twice with the palm to his face while keeping control of his lead hand, take him down with an ankle Kick Throw

2

Stop-kick the assailant in the ribs as he develops his punching attacks; follow-up with a Throat Strike and a Groin Kick; then a Circular Elbow Strike that turns into an Outer Reap Takedown; finish him up with a Stomp to the ribs

THE PUSHING SIDE STOP KICK

9. THE LOW SIDE KICK

This is the most practical version of the Side Kick, and one of the most useful in Self-defense. It was, reportedly, *Bruce Lee*'s favorite Kick, used as an Obstruction Kick, a Stop Kick or an Offensive Attack Kick. We have seen a few examples in the previous section, and the principles are identical to those of the execution of the higher version to the hips or ribs.

The technical Low Side Kick

The Low Side Kick is a perfect obstruction maneuver to help you get safely close to the opponent and start your Retzev

The Kick is quite stealthy, very powerful, very fast and it targets the very sensitive *knee or upper shin*. Krav Maga uses the front-leg version with minimal chambering. It concentrates on **speed** and on the **penetration** of the target: you must kick fast and a few inches '*into*' the knee joint.

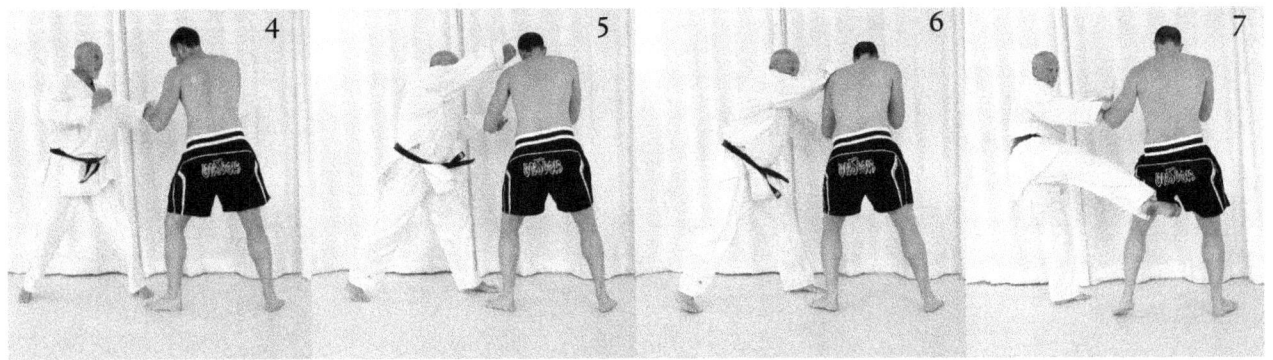

Kick a few inches into the knee

Like with all Low Kicks (and even all Kicks), you should drill a *stealthy delivery*: making sure that the upper body does not give any hint of the impending and developing attack. Drill in front of the mirror.

The only important target is the knee joint, from all possible angles, but you must learn to kick 'through' and not just slap the surface of the knee. The upper shin can be a target if the opponent's leg is straight, and the lower thigh can be a target for the Stop version of the Kick. But you should drill the automatic targeting of the knee at all times.

Preempt a stick attack with a Hopping Low Stop side kick to the knee; follow-up with another hard Low Side kick and start your Retzev...

Release from a two-handed wrist grab followed by a Low Side Kick counter and a finger whip to the eyes; keep attacking until the opponent is neutralized

"A righteous man falls down seven times and gets up."
~King Solomon, Proverbs, 24:16.

THE LOW SIDE KICK

10. THE STOMPING SIDE KICK

The Stomping Side Kick is identical to the regular Low Side Kick until the moment of impact. From then on, instead of penetrating for a few inches and then chambering back, it keeps going down and 'through' *until it reaches the floor and crushes the knee into it.* This is a debilitating attack, generally directed at the back of the knee. It works as well when attacking the sides of the knee, and it is then even more damaging for the joint. Attacking the front knee of a straightened leg is also an option, but it is an extremely dangerous Kick, with the potential of causing lifelong serious injuries. Be careful in training and in actual use if warranted. It is certainly not for the faint-hearted.

The Stomping Side Kick: simple but devastating

Kick all the way to the ground, and more

KRAV MAGA KICKS

It is an important kick to master for self-preservation, and it should be drilled as an all-the-way technique, kicking through and stomping forcefully. Use old tires, focus pads, bags and more for realistic power development.

Use props to drill the 'kick-through

The best way to 'understand' the Kick is to drill applications, like the few ones presented below.

A great kick when you are suddenly accosted from your side...

...or if you can 'get' the opponent's back

THE STOMPING SIDE KICK

It is also a crippling 'Cutting Kick', crushing the knee of the standing leg of a kicking assailant. Evade and kick...

...or Block/Catch and kick!

Of course, the kick can be an excellent offensive maneuver. It can be used simply directly.

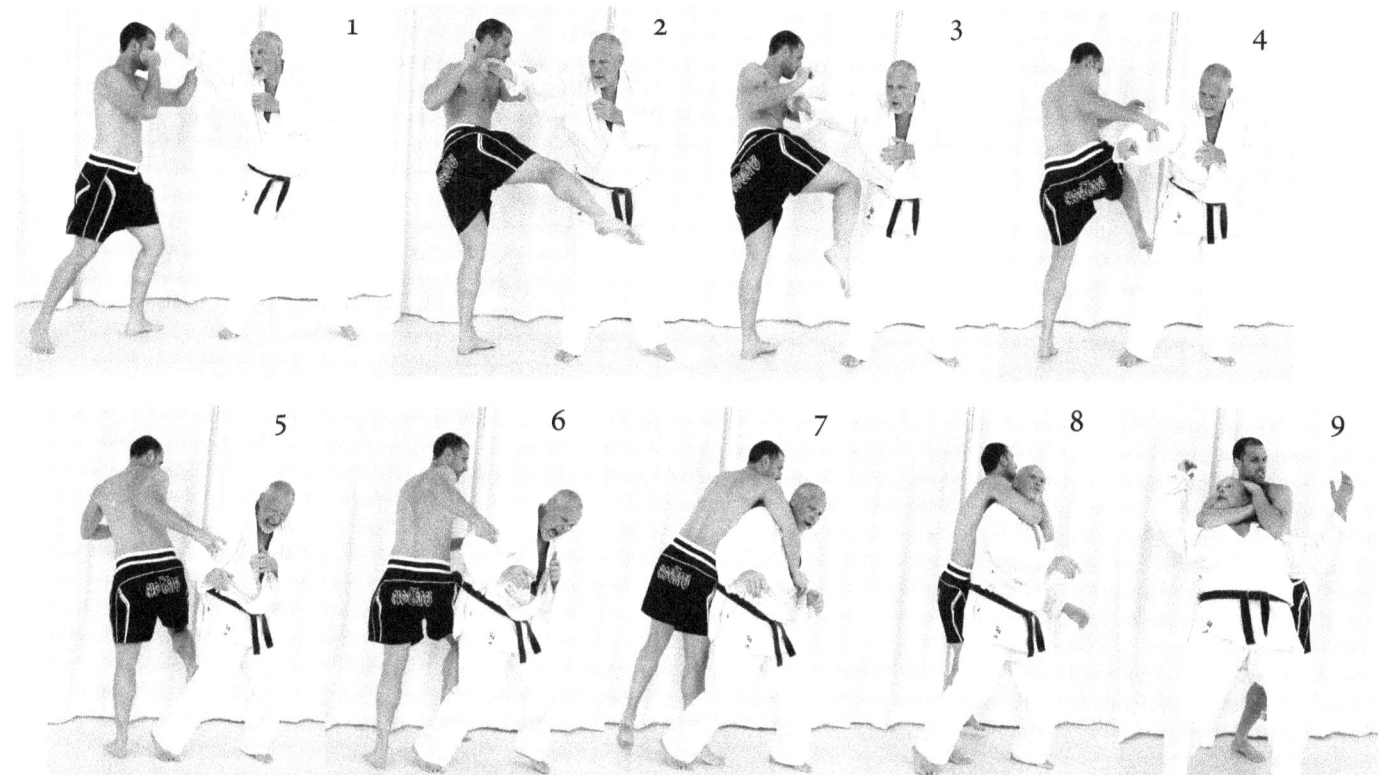

The kick is as useful in the midst of a defensive combination, generally with a forward diagonal evasion. The technique lends itself to pretty mean follow-ups

Another defensive combination with a hard finish

THE STOMPING SIDE KICK

The Stomping Low Kick is also the technique of choice if you must intervene to save a loved one from an assault. Stomping the back of the knee will stop the most determined assailant; of course, keep the *Retzev* if necessary.

The kick of choice to protect a third party

11. The Small Roundhouse Kick

The 'Small' Roundhouse Kick is *Krav Maga*'s Circular Kick. It attacks the sides of an attacker standing in front of you. It differs from Martial Arts' **'Full'** Roundhouse with its restricted chambering in front of the body. This 'small' chambering allows for much more speed and for a more protected execution; it is much less powerful than the 'Full' version though. But in *Krav Maga*, we shall nearly exclusively target the testicles or the front knee, and power is therefore a secondary consideration. But, the <u>serious drilling</u> of this 'Small' version of the Roundhouse Kick will allow to add serious power to the move and then allow for eventually targeting the solar plexus, the lower ribs and the lower back (or the head of a kneeling opponent). All these secondary targets will be made even more vulnerable if you happen to wear hard-soled or hard-tipped shoes.

Karate's Full version of the Roundhouse Kick: powerful but slower and unprotected

*The **Small** Roundhouse Kick, better suited for Krav Maga*

Target the groin area

Targeting the lower back and kidneys area

Target the head of a threatening kneeling or standing-up opponent

The Roundhouse Kick is a versatile bread-and-butter Kick and it needs to be drilled in its rear-leg, in its <u>front-leg</u> and in its <u>hopping-forward</u> version. It even has also a great <u>Body-bent</u> version (just like the Side Kick) so important that it will have its own section. Roundhouse Kicks are 'Whipping' Kicks and the fast and powerful *chambering back* is very important to success. But even more important is **penetration**: do not make the mistake of turning this Kick into a 'slap' surface kick. Before chambering back, it is imperative to kick forcefully *a few inches into* the target. Do not start to slow down before impact for a better pull back. <u>Accelerate until contact and go through before whipping back!</u>

The rear-leg version of the Small Roundhouse

The front-leg Hopping version; note that the hop happens while the leg is already chambering

All of the above are reasons why this Kick must be drilled for **speed and 'kick-through'** against a focus pad held by a partner. It should also be drilled for automatic going to the opponent's **groin** when in range, and this in the **stealthiest** way possible (no upper body telegraphing). Drill, drill, drill! A few illustrative Applications will follow.

Drill the Kick with a partner holding a focus pad to learn to kick 'into' the target (No need to kick high though)

KRAV MAGA KICKS

An Offensive application of the front-leg Hopping version: lunge to catch his front wrist, in order to draw his attention away from the targeted groin and to neutralize a possible blocking or countering han

An Offensive application of the more powerful rear-leg version: Draw his attention up with a lunging Jab, and kick the groin; follow up with a Low Kick to the knee, and keep going

It is also a great Preemptive Kick: kick the assailant's groin in the middle of his kicking hop forward; again, start you following Retzev with a Low Kick to the knee

THE SMALL ROUNDHOUSE KICK   63

The Hopping front-leg version is a surprising Preemptive Kick because it is unexpectedly going forward towards an attacking opponent; for example, in an overhead stick attack

Also a great Defensive Kick: after evading out a Punch

Defensive Kick against a Kick: block an deflect the opponent's kick in order to powerfully roundhouse-kick the knee of the attacking leg; you could follow up by 'owning' his back for a Stomp in back of same knee and a Knee Strike to the head you are pulling violently back and down

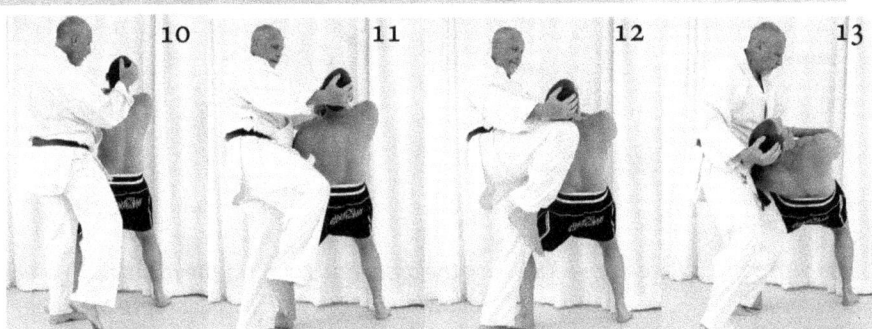

64   **KRAV MAGA KICKS**

12. The Bent-body Long Roundhouse Kick

This version of the Small Roundhouse Kick has its own section because of its importance. Bending away while developing the Groin Roundhouse Kick has the same advantage as for the Side Kick: it keeps your head and trunk away from attacks or counterattacks. It makes the kick safer. But, for the Roundhouse Kick, it also allows for a hip push during execution. This hip push, together with bending the standing leg, gives the Kick a longer range. Hence the 'Long' in **Body-bent Long Roundhouse Kick**. This execution of the Kick is surprisingly long, and therefore it will more easily hit the opponent's groin. Longer, safer; what is not to like?

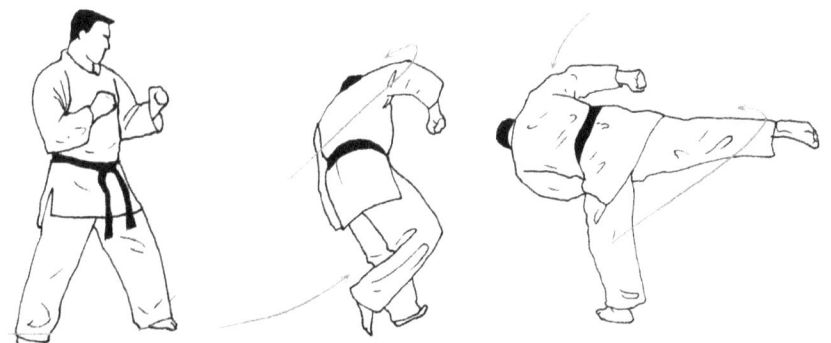

The Bent-body Long Roundhouse Kick

The 'Hand-on-floor' version

The *Krav Maga* target for this kick should be nearly exclusively the opponent's **testicles**. The only other option would be the lower back at kidneys level, and this only with the more powerful rear-leg version. In both cases, it is imperative to kick a few inches _into_ the target, then to chamber back brusquely, and finally to follow up aggressively.

The rear-leg version to the lower back; note how the bent body keeps you safe

An Offensive application of the rear-leg version to the lower back: start with a high Jab/Cross to 'open' his lower back and follow up with a Whipping Punch and an Outer Reap Takedown

An aggressive Preemptive Kick to the groin will surprise a threatening armed assailant; of course, you need to keep the pressure: Body-bent Side Kick through the knee, Punch to the nose, rear-leg Roundhouse to the groin again, Sweep,...

All in all: A great Kick worth drilling!

KRAV MAGA KICKS

13. The 'Low Kick' or Straight-leg Roundhouse

The Straight-leg Low Circular Kick is a classic of 'hard' Martial Arts like *Kyokushinkai Karate, Muay Thai Boxing and MMA* among others. It is so classic that it has earned the common name of 'Low Kick'. This is a Power Kick in which you give 'everything you have'.

Unlike the Roundhouse Kick it is not a 'Whipping' Kick and it does not require a chamber-back: you kick through the target all the way. The target, in *Krav Maga*, is exclusively the knee. Kicking the upper thigh, like in sporting versions, is not good enough for self-preservation: it will usually be enough to stop an amateurish assailant, but it risks not being enough for a trained adversary, a hardened criminal in high adrenalin state or an opponent on drugs. Therefore, the *Krav Maga* trainee is invited to drill attacking the knee exclusively, so as not to miss it if ever in a stressful real world situation.

The Low Kick

The Kick requires using the hips to 'pull' the near-straight leg in an arc directly through the target. It is the shoulders that start to pivot, pulling in the trunk and the hips like an elastic band that will then launch the leg explosively. Once the Kick is launched, the hips start spinning in the opposite direction. You should aim to kick through the side of the opponent's knee, inside or outside, and *start decelerating only at least a foot behind the target*. One cannot stress enough that it is a kick-through maneuver with no afterthought or hesitation. Muay Thai fighters often make a full circle after the kick, instead of slowing the momentum after impact (Muay Thai fighters also step out diagonally with the front foot to 'open' the hips before pulling the Kick).

The Low Kick: pivot with the hips first, then kick through!

 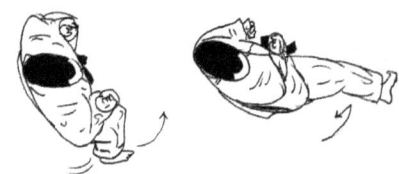 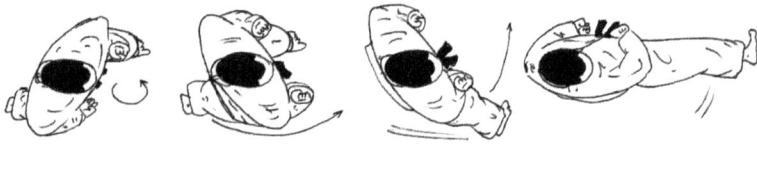

Sky View comparison of the Low Kick (up) to the classic Roundhouse (down)

Drill the kick for power and precision; note the twist of the hips before execution

This is a very aggressive maneuver and it should be drilled as one. You should project your body and mind forward with the idea of crushing your opponent with everything you have. It can be used as an <u>All-purpose Stop Kick</u> if you have the required mental attitude: Wait to 'feel' the very beginning of your opponent's attack and jump forward with an all-powerful 'Low Kick' at knee's height. Your attacker expects you to retreat or stay in place to block; instead you are disturbing his range expectations, jamming his attack and kicking through his moving legs with everything you have got. Ouch! Follow up!
This Kick requires serious **power training on the heavy bag**. After lots of drilling, you will have in your arsenal a Kick that can single-handedly win a fight. Really: One Kick to the knee; end of fight.

Various applications are presented below, but it is truly a versatile All-purpose Kick, always suitable.

Feint and step slightly out (Muay Thai-style) to kick through the inside knee

68   KRAV MAGA KICKS

Setting up a Low Kick to the outside knee with a low to high Progressive Indirect Punching Attack (PIA)

The simplest Low Kick set-up: High Jab/Cross to Low Kick

Aggressive Counter after a Leg Block: Double Low Kick to the same knee, inside and outside

THE 'LOW KICK'

14. THE PENETRATING BACK KICK

The Penetrating Back Kick is even more powerful than the Side Kick, because it adds the power of the glutes to that of the lower back, but it has the disadvantage to be, at least partially, executed while presenting your back to the opponent. But it can be a great Kick in a dynamic situation. Just imagine you have missed with a 'Low Kick' and your momentum has taken you too far: instead of coming back to face him, use a Powerful Back Kick.

The *Krav Maga Back Kick* does not require the full chamber of traditional Martial Arts: the Kick is so powerful that it can do with a minimal chambering. The important point will be to kick with the hips and to bend forward (45 degrees) for maximum power at impact. Chambering back remains important though.

The classic Penetrating Back Kick with full chamber

A powerful Kick indeed!

The Back Kick is difficult to use with absolute precision; that is why it usually targets the center of the body. The good news is that it is so powerful that it will do damage anywhere it connects. Aim for the *lower abdomen, the hips, the ribs and even the solar plexus*. If you are very proficient and can be more precise, then you should aim for the **groin** area, and even the **knee**.

Aiming for the general groin area is a good policy

The Kick is obviously to be used to strike an opponent who is behind you, whether he is attacking you from behind or whether you have presented your back (by accident or purposely). In Krav Maga, you can also **spin forward** to get into position for a powerful Back Kick.

The classic Spin-forward Back Kick

The classic Back Kick against an assailant from behind you

The Spin-forward Back Kick allows you to attack the groin of an opponent in a well-guarded side stance

THE PENETRATING BACK KICK

The Spinning-back Back Kick is **not** recommended for basic *Krav Maga* training: it is oversophisticated for stressed real-life use and it requires lots of training to avoid the diagonal trajectory caused by the mix of a circular spin-back and a straight kick. *Unless very proficient*, forget about it.

On the other hand, if you have spinned (back or forward), by accident, momentum or on purpose, and then have stopped, you could be in good position for a Back Kick. This would not be a Spin-back Back Kick *per se*, but a regular Back Kick after a completed pivot.

The classic Spin-back Back Kick: not recommended for the Kravist

The Back Kick is a powerful and very versatile Kick that can be and should be used any time you have your back partly or fully towards the opponent.
And the best follow-up to a Back Kick is nearly always … another Back Kick!

Two Back Kicks in series

KRAV MAGA KICKS

15. The Short Back Kick

The importance of Back Kicks is that they can be executed against an assailant behind you, whether he attacks you from behind or whether the fight places you in such a relative situation. The Penetrating Back Kick above is very useful and powerful if you find yourself in such a situation. But it does not work if your adversary is too close behind you.

If such is the case, you have to change the trajectory of the Kick: instead of going straight behind you, it arches outwards as much as necessary to allow for a power-gathering vector. The execution requires some flexibility, and certainly requires serious drilling on the heavy bag. It is important tough, because you never know when you can find yourself in such a situation. Only drilling will make you familiar with the Kick and will allow you to pack it with necessary power.

The classic Short Back kick

Applied Short Back kick

The Ultra-short Back kick from very close up

The Krav Maga targets of this Kick are essentially the *groin, the lower abdomen and the lower ribs.* Most of what has been said for the regular Penetrating Back Kick stays valid for this short version.

Short Back Kick and elbowing follow-up, after a Leg Block that presents your back partly to the opponent

Offensive Combination with a Spin-back Short Back kick, by an expert

16. THE UPWARD BACK KICKS

Uppercut Back kick, Upward Hook Back Kick and Ghost Back Kick

The other and preferred option if your attacker is behind you and is close, is to use a Back Kick with an *Upward trajectory* that targets... the testicles. These Kicks could also target the face of a bent-over opponent, but not really in *Krav Maga* where numerous more serious options are available.

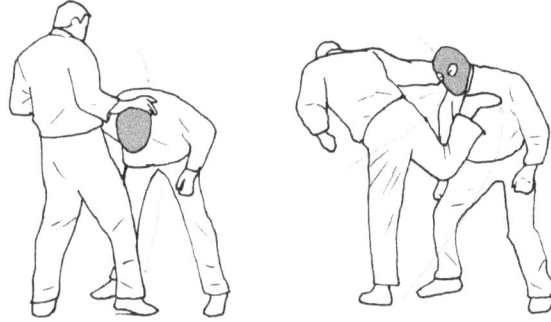

Uppercut Back Kick to the face, not really a classic Krav Maga move

The Uppercut Back Kick simply travels straight up into the groin with the bottom of the foot up. It is imperative to kick up a few inches *into* the target *with the idea of lifting the opponent up*. Then follow up.

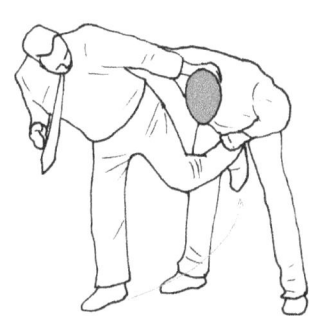

Applied Uppercut Back Kick after a high block

Feint to provoke a counter and Uppercut-kick the groin of the kicking opponent

THE UPWARD BACK KICKS

The Upward Hook Back Kick is more devastating, but it requires that the legs of the opponent be at least slightly open. The idea is to kick with the heel behind the testicles, and then 'hook' into them by pulling the foot back forward; all the while you are kicking a few inches up into the target. This hits the area hard (heel) and then pulls the testicles violently forward. It is a very easy technique to master and a very debilitating move, but it requires to be close to the opponent, as you have to kick between his legs, behind his crotch. It should be noted that the technique can also be executed from behind the opponent.

The classic 'hooking' Back Kick to the testicles

The trajectory and effect of the Kick

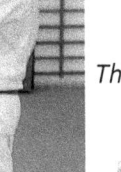

Another view of the Hooking Back groin Kick

The Hooking Back Kick executed from behind the opponent

Applied Hooking Back Kick from behind

The Ghost Back Kick is more a 'trick' than a full-fledged technique. It is surprisingly effective though, because it is stealthy and it makes use of the bully psychology of most attackers. In this maneuver, you turn your back to your assailant as if cowering and getting ready to flee. While it emboldens him and neutralizes caution, your (formerly) front foot simply goes up into his approaching groin. Surprise! And then you follow up, immediately and reinstate your **aggressive** 'no-victim' posture.

The Ghost Back Kick, simple but effective

Applied Ghost Back Kick after an offensive opening

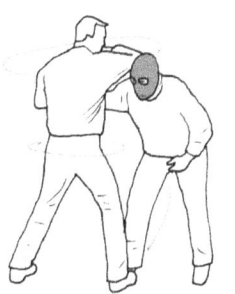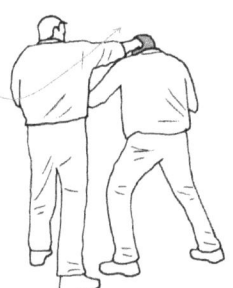

Feint cowering from a stick strike, ghost-back-kick and...Retzev

17. THE SMALL HEEL BACK HOOK KICK

If your opponent is behind you, but stands sideways, you will not have access to his groin with straight or upward Back Kicks. **The Small Heel Back Hook Kick** is the solution. This is a very fast, relatively easy, generally unexpected and deceivingly powerful Kick that has the added advantage of allowing some 'hooking' into the groin. It is a hybrid between a Hook Kick and a Back Kick that should be drilled by every fighter. It should be drilled on the marked (*at groin level*) heavy bag for power and penetration: touch the bag behind you for distance and kick with minimal upper body movement. Try to kick without looking, or looking only just before impact: it should be an explosive Stealth Kick.

The Small Heel Back Hook Kick

Sky View of the Kick

The applied Kick

KRAV MAGA KICKS

The Photos and Drawings show hitting the opponent's ribs, but, in *Krav Maga*, the Kick should only target the **groin** area. Kick into the target and 'hook in' with your heel.

In Krav Maga, one should target the groin and not the ribs as illustrated

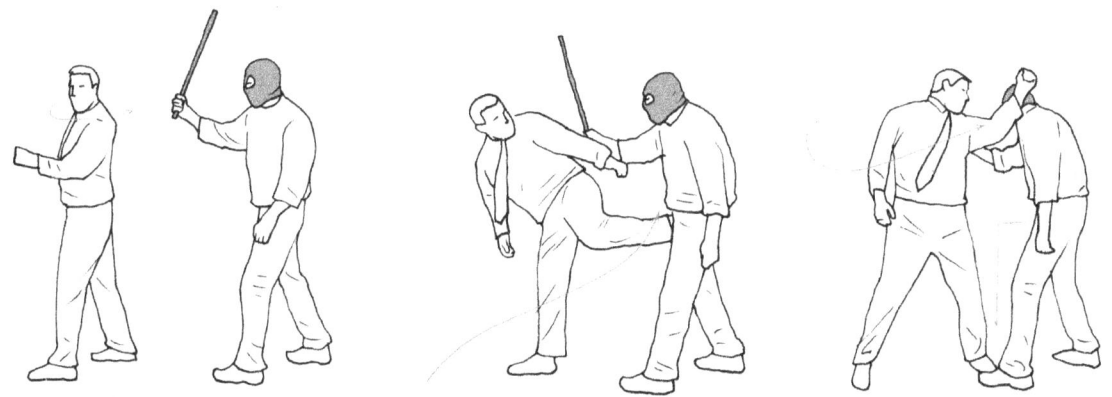
pplied Small Heel Back Hook Kick against threatening attacker from behind; always follow up

Offensive application of the Kick; the Krav Maga version should target the groin

18. THE CRESCENT KICK

The Crescent Kick is not very versatile. In *Krav Maga*, it would not be used for anything else than hitting the elbow of the opponent's arm. It is a very powerful Kick, but it requires gathering power along its trajectory and is not very practical for the below-the-belt sensitive-target parameters of Krav Maga. It could be used to powerfully kick through the head of a bent-over opponent, or to kick the groin area of an adversary in perfect relative side position; but those are not especially common situations.

The (Inside) Crescent Kick

The trainee is just invited to drill the Kick as a kick-through powerful attack of the lead limb of the opponent. Being a very good fitness drill as well, it can only do good.
Aim for the *elbow* as precisely as possible and use the effect at impact to follow-up aggressively.

Crescent Kick to the elbow joint; follow up!

Two Crescent Kicks to the opponent's elbows in an aggressive combination: elbow joints destruction tactic

<u>This Kick is not to be used in its Hollywood version: crescent-kicking the knife-armed (or even gun-armed) wrist of an assailant is tantamount to suicide! Remember that!</u>

19. The Outside Crescent kick

Everything said about the Crescent Kick is valid for *the Outside Crescent Kick*, including and especially the Hollywood warning part. The only difference between the kicks is the opposite trajectory.

Front view of the Outside Crescent Kick

Side view of the Outside Crescent kick

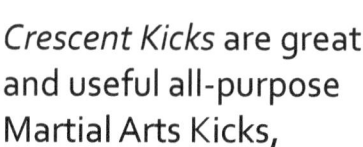

Crescent Kicks are great and useful all-purpose Martial Arts Kicks, but they are not in line with *Krav Maga* principles. They can just be used for blocking attacking limbs and for elbow destruction.

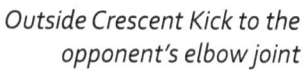

Outside Crescent Kick to the opponent's elbow joint

  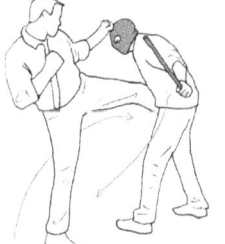 

Attack the stick-brandishing elbow and follow up

THE OUTSIDE CRESCENT KICK

20. The Outward Ghost Groin Kick

This is a fantastic little Kick, easy to perform and extremely effective. It should be a nearly automatic Kick if you find yourself close to the opponent, especially if you are interested in kicking and then keep moving away from the situation.

The Applied Outward Ghost Groin Kick

The Outward Ghost Groin kick

The classic execution of the kick

A great offensive technique to move away from an opponent, for example in the case of multiple attackers

82 **KRAV MAGA KICKS**

In *Krav Maga*, the Kick will be essentially directed at the *groin* (Other Martial Arts also target the solar plexus, the inside knee and the head of a bent-over opponent). What makes it formidable is that it does not need to be precise, but just powerful and in the general area. The reverberation of the shock wave in the general genital area will do the work. *But it also means that this Kick should be seriously drilled for power on focus pads and on the hanging bag.*

The Kick is easy to execute and understand, but more difficult to explain in words. The reader is invited to refer to the Photos and Drawings. The key points for success with this technique are:
- *commitment* (no hesitation),
- keeping the upper body as disconnected as possible for as long as possible to *avoid telegraphing* the move,
- the execution of the kick *with the hips and the whole body*,
- and kicking *through* the opponent, all the way.

You can then either follow-up or keep going away from your withering opponent, according to the situation.

A few self-explanatory applications follow. Just remember to drill the Kick for power and for a stealthy execution. The fact that it looks simple does not mean you can scrounge on the training.

The Kick in a wrist grab self-defense move with follow-up

The Kick at the end of an offensive combination

THE OUTWARD GHOST GROIN KICK

The Outward Ghost Groin kick is also a great Stop Kick: just kick go towards the attack and kick through with everything you have. Here illustrated against a front-leg kicking opponent!

This Kick requires serious drilling in order to become a true 'doomsday' weapon; here training on the focus pad

Drilling for power and penetration on the heavy bag

KRAV MAGA KICKS

PART 2

Krav Maga - Vulnerable Points to Target

נקודות התורפה

The late Sidney Shlomo Faiga, Roy Faiga and Marc De Bremaeker, respectively, in a Krav Maga demo. 1980ies.

Krav Maga's Vulnerable Points to Target

One of the main attributes of *Krav Maga* is the <u>exclusive targeting of vulnerable points</u>. This is a no-nonsense fighting system that is supposed to work in stressful situations. Unless you are a lifelong dedicated Martial Artist, hitting esoteric pressure points or striking the opponent randomly does not work. One must also bear in mind that in high adrenalin-state, feelings of pain are dulled and therefore an assailant's body can easily take much more punishment that you can imagine from your armchair.

By concentrating on a limited number of targets, *Krav Maga* makes the acquisition of good habits and effective techniques much simpler: you can drill the maneuvers many more times and you will basically often execute the same strikes in different 'Retzev' all the time. These automatisms will serve you right when your body will be on autopilot in a stressful 'real world' situation.

Krav Maga is also not for the faint-hearted; it is a system developed for survival in warfare and in life-threatening situations. Survival trumps all social norms, and training is required for a normative citizen to acquire self-preserving reflexes that are not in line with his social education and background.

We will describe here the main **Vulnerable Points** to target in training (*carefully*) and in case of need (*at full power*). The targets mentioned in this book are not restricted to those you should kick; all main targets will be mentioned. They can be kicked, punched, palm-striked, elbowed, kneed, and even bitten if your survival depends on it…

"If you find yourself in a fair fight, you didn't plan your mission properly."
~Colonel David Hackworth

1. First Line Targets

The First Line Targets that must be hit with priority whenever possible are:

1. The Groin
2. The Groin
3. The Groin.

This pun is intended to underline the importance of the *testicles* and of the general *groin area* as a vulnerable point to strike in a survival situation.

I once had a Tai Jitsu instructor, very good but rather foul-mouthed, that used to say: "In real combat, you do not have an opponent, you have a floating pair of balls in front of you". This is a quote and I apologize for the language; but it expresses very clearly the state of mind required and the importance of making targeting the groin a second nature.

You can and should hit the groin from the front, from the back, with your feet, with your knees, with your palms, with your elbows, with your head; you can even try to grab them…

The testicles are an exception to the adrenalin-pumped pain theory: nearly everyone will experience excruciating pain when hit. The physical damage is also very serious. But this does not mean that you have to stop your '*Retzev*' after a successful groin strike. Remember that *Krav Maga* series do not stop until the opponent is fully neutralized; you may need to repeat the groin strike, follow with other strikes to sensitive targets, or destroy the assailant's joints to make sure the danger to you or your loved ones is over.

KRAV MAGA KICKS

Krav Maga first line targets

FIRST LINE TARGETS

2. Second Line Targets

The Second Line Targets must be targeted when the groin is well protected, out of reach, or has already been hit, or has been feinted towards to elicit a reaction. *Second Line Targets* are crippling targets, but they still have always to be part of a 'Retzev' and followed up until complete victory.
Unlike in traditional Martial Arts, they are not pinpointed vulnerable points to be struck with precision and with specific natural weapons: They are general areas rich in such points! *Krav Maga* takes into account the stress of real life threats for normative people not used to violence. It would be difficult for them in such situations to react with pinpoint precision!

The Secondary Targets List reads as follows:

2.1 The Nose ('Middle of the Face' Target).
The *nose* is a great target: easy to find in the middle of the face, and very sensitive. When you hit someone's nose hard, you overload his senses: shock his sense of touch with the impact, blurr his vision with the watering of his eyes, disturb his ability to breathe through the nose, and make him smell and taste blood,... The preferred kicking weapons are the *knee* or the *top of the foot* when you have caused him to bend forward, and the *bottom of the foot* if he is already on the floor. The preferred punching weapons are the *fist* and the *palm of the hand*, although *elbows* and *head* butts are not to be sneezed at. The author tends to prefer the Palm to the Fist for *2 reasons*:
- it is safer to the fingers, especially in stressed situations where the fist is not necessarily well-rolled.
- it has the fingers visiting the area around the opponent's eyes, which is very disturbing to the attacked.

The nose is also a great target, because, being in the middle of the face, it lends itself to misses that are still good targets: the eyes and orbital bone, the cheekbones, the lips,... Of course, after scoring on the nose, you have to keep hitting until your assailant is fully subdued.

Head Butt to the nose

Knee Strike to the nose

2.2 The Throat (Adam's Apple and the general Larynx area).

The **throat** is not always easy to reach, but when possible, it is a crippling target, even to the extent of being lethal. This, of course, underlines the need for utmost caution in training and in actual 'real world' use. If your life is not in danger, you should avoid targeting the throat; this is not for stopping an inebriated acquaintance fooling around! A crushed larynx will cause breathing difficulty that can lead to asphyxiation and death. On the other hand, if your life is in danger from several real thugs or an armed mugger, you should use your *knuckles*, the *sword edge of your hand*, the *webbed part between your thumb and forefingers* or the *sword edge of your foot* to strike the throat. If you miss slightly, you are still in a sensitive target-rich environment: the chin, the carotids, the lips and the clavicles.

Knuckle Strike to the throat

Striking the throat with the weapon seized from the attacker

2.3 The Eyes (and the Orbital Cavity Ridge).

The **eyes** are an obvious but often underused target. Poking the eyes is, of course, a very painful and crippling move that can cause blindness. Poking with the *straightened fingers* or *protruding knuckles* is a very serious and dangerous technique to be used only in life-threatening circumstances. But the eyes can also be attacked in serious but milder ways: you can punch or palm-strike the *general eye area* to damage the orbital cavity, or you can **rake or whip-strike** the eyes to cause an atavistic reaction that will include lifting the hands (and therefore uncover the primary target). The <u>Whipping Strike towards the eyes</u> is an extremely fast and effective technique to be used any time possible; it has milder consequences than a poke, but it as effective in the very short term needed. When you are going with a Punch or a Palm Strike for the general eye area, you are in a good neighborhood: should you miss, you still could hit the nose, the temple or the higher cheekbone.

Fingers Poke to the eyes

2.4 The Back of the Neck (Cervical vertebrae).

The **Back of the neck** is a potentially crippling target that can even cause death. Be extremely careful in training and in real-life use. In the unfortunate life-preserving circumstances, it must be struck with a penetrating blow *that goes through*. The weapons used are the *knife of the hand*, the *elbow*, the *forearm*, and in the right set-up the *foot*. We cannot underline enough the seriousness of striking the cervical area: be wise and calculated.

SECOND LINE TARGETS

Elbow strike to the back of the neck

2.5 The Knees.

The **knee** is an important target: it is easy to reach, especially if your opponent has a high guard to protect his face or if you have provoked his lifting his hands, for example with a feint towards his eyes. The knee should be hit from any side possible: front, back and sides: it is a very sensitive joint. Most serious kicks will damage the knee, cause pain and hamper the assailant's mobility; their crippling potential should also be understood. The knee can be attacked with straight, circular and stomping Kicks; one has just to remember to kick *through* the target. No surface-slapping!

It is also important to target the knee with *precision*: the traditional 'Low Kick' (*Circular*) is usually delivered to the thigh; it hurts but it is a bad self-defense habit. Go for the knee with precision, because you want to destroy the ability of your attacker to move and to stand.

Stomping the knee

Krav Maga's Secondary Targets

SECOND LINE TARGETS

3. Third Line Targets

Attacking the **tertiary targets** is damaging and painful, but not easily crippling. Striking them will nevertheless cause a shock to be used for following up in the *Retzev*, preferably towards the groin or at least towards more serious secondary targets. Hitting these sensitive points causes physiological reactions that will (1) hurt the opponent, (2) add to the overall shock of the previous strikes and (3) give you enough time (in milliseconds) to keep attacking without allowing for a counter. *Tertiary targets are always part of a Retzev, as a transition or as a distracting move (leading to something else).*

Here comes the Tertiary Targets List:

3.1 The Side of the Face.

This 'target' goes from the *temple* through the *ear* all the way to the *mandibular joint* (jaw hinge). The *temple* could be a secondary target if it was not difficult to pinpoint exactly in a stressful situation: a collapsed temporal area is crippling and can even be fatal. The *ears* are full of sensitive nerve endings and can tear easily, but the best way to attack them is with a *Palm Strike* (preferably Twin Strike to both ears) that will tear the eardrum (*tympan*) and cause a serious loss of balance control. Remember not to 'slap' but to strike forcefully through the target, like always. If you miss the ears and strike the hinge of the jaw, no big deal: it is very painful and can cause a serious dislocation that will win you the fight. The weapons of choice for the Side of the Face area are: the *Palm*, the *Knife-hand*, the *forearm* and the *elbow*; of course the *knee*, the *top of the foot*, the *tip of your shoe* and the *fist* are valid as well.

Palm Strike to the side of the face

The concussing Ears Twin Palm Strike: simple but very damaging

3.2 The Side of the Neck (Carotids and Vertebrae).

The **side of the neck** is a good target because of the veins and carotid arteries, as well as many nerve endings. You must strike powerfully 'into' the target and not just 'slap' the surface. By doing so, you will also shake the cervical vertebrae. This sensitive target can be attacked with the *Knife-hand*, the *forearm*, the *elbow*, the *palm*, the *fist* and the *foot*. Should you miss slightly because of your opponent moving, you would still probably strike the side of the head, the back of the neck, the throat or the clavicle...

Knife-hand Strike to the side of the neck   another type of Knife-hand Strike to the side of the neck   Another side-of-the-neck strike

3.3 The Collarbone (Clavicle).

The **clavicles** are an underused target: these are bones that are relatively easy to break, which is very painful, causes serious internal damage and basically takes the corresponding shoulder out of the game immediately. The ideal point to strike, diagonally from above, is at about one third of its length from the throat side, but anywhere will be very effective and reverberate from the shoulder all the way to the neck. The collarbone can be attacked with the *fist*, the *hammer-fist*, the *forearm*, the *elbow*, the *Knife-hand*, and, in the right set-up, with any part of the *foot*.

3.4 The Solar Plexus (Celiac plexus).

This network of nerves at the pit of the stomach is very sensitive to a reverberating strike; it is close to the stomach and the aorta. The general area to target is in the middle of the trunk just below the chest-bone (*sternum*). On top of being very painful, a strong blow causes the diaphragm to spasm, and hence difficulty in breathing. It can also affect the nerve plexus itself and damage the viscera. Knocking the wind out of an opponent will, of course, allow you to follow up easily. Pinpointing the exact *solar plexus* point is not always easy in stressful situations, but a powerful penetrating strike in the general area will generally be good enough. Kick with any part of the foot, but kick 'into' the target. The *straightened fingers*, the *knuckles*, the *fist*, the *elbow* and the *knee* will make good penetrating weapons too. The *head* and the *palm* can also be used if their striking trajectory comes from below or straight on (not from above).

3.5 The Floating Ribs (False and Floating Ribs).

The term '*floating ribs*' is loosely used in Martial Arts, as it usually also includes the so-called 'False Ribs'. The False Ribs (Ribs 8 to 10) are so called because they are not directly attached to the chest bone (sternum), but are so through a cartilage link to the 'Real' Ribs above them. The Floating Ribs (Ribs 11 and 12) are not attached at all to the sternum in any way. The common denominator is that they both are 'weak' ribs that do not protect very well the internal organs under them. Moreover, well-delivered Kicks can easily cause damage to the ribs themselves. You can also use the *knee*, the *fist*, the *elbow* and the *forearm*.

Lower back Kick

3.6 The Kidneys (Lower Back Area)

Kicking the **lower back area** is very efficient: it is painful and causes a disturbing concussion that will open the assailant to easier follow-ups. You should kick '*into*' the general area just above the belt: it encompasses the sensitive kidneys, but also the vertebrae. A powerful Strike will reverberate along the whole of the spine and into the lower internal organs like the liver. It also often kicks the wind out of the opponent because the shock causes the diaphragm to contract. Pinpointing the *kidneys* with the *knee*, the *fist* or the *hammer-fist* is possible, but targeting this area is more the realm of a kick, especially the Circular Kicks connecting with the *ankle* or the *shin*.

3.7 The Elbow Joints.

Striking the **elbow joint** with power can destroy the opponent's ability to keep fighting, but breaking the elbow will only come if you strike the elbow of an extended arm from outside while keeping the wrist in place. Most regular strikes to the elbow will numb and cause pain to allow for a follow-up. Remember to strike *through* the elbow, all the way. Use the *Knife-hand*, the *forearm* or the *crescent kick* presented in Part One. The other good way to destroy the opponent's elbow to prevent further attacks, is to <u>stomp</u> the elbow of an opponent on the ground, which is entirely justifiable in the case of a life-saving situation (especially against an armed assailant).

Elbow Break attempt: Knife-hand Strike while keeping the forearm in place

3.8 The Hands (*Wrist and Fingers*).

Damaging the opponent's **hands** will prevent his ability and will to keep on fighting. That goes without saying. Striking the wrist of an assailant with the *knife-hand* or the *forearm* can rattle him, but the best way to take the attacking hands out is to stomp on them when the opponent is on the ground. Do not hesitate: crushed fingers are very painful and will seriously diminish your opponent's abilities and belligerence.

3.9 The Feet (*Ankles to toes*).

What is true for the hands/wrists/fingers is doubly true for the **ankles/feet/toes**. The only differences are: that you can (1) crush those also when your attacker is still standing, and (2) that a damaged foot will hamper the opponent's ability to move and stand. Foot Stomping is an underused maneuver, which makes it usually more surprising. It is very easy to perform and fiendishly effective. You should do it nearly automatically whenever possible. The only drawback is that it requires you to be close to the opponent. But if you find yourself close for any reason, go for it...

3.10 The shin (*Tibia and Fibula Bones*).

The **shins** also undeservedly make for underused targets. The shins are very rich in nerve endings and the shinbone is pretty prone to damage. Kicking the shins is also pretty easy to do with fast kicks, if you execute them stealthily without moving the upper body, or if you kick just after feinting high with the hands. Kicking the shins is always a great opener, or a fantastic diversion before a decisive attack; it is extremely efficient if you have *hard-tipped shoe*s. Shin Splints and Stress Fractures will be the mildest results of a hard-soled shoe striking 'through' the tibia. Drill the Kick and use it whenever possible.

Kicking the sensitive shins. With shoes!

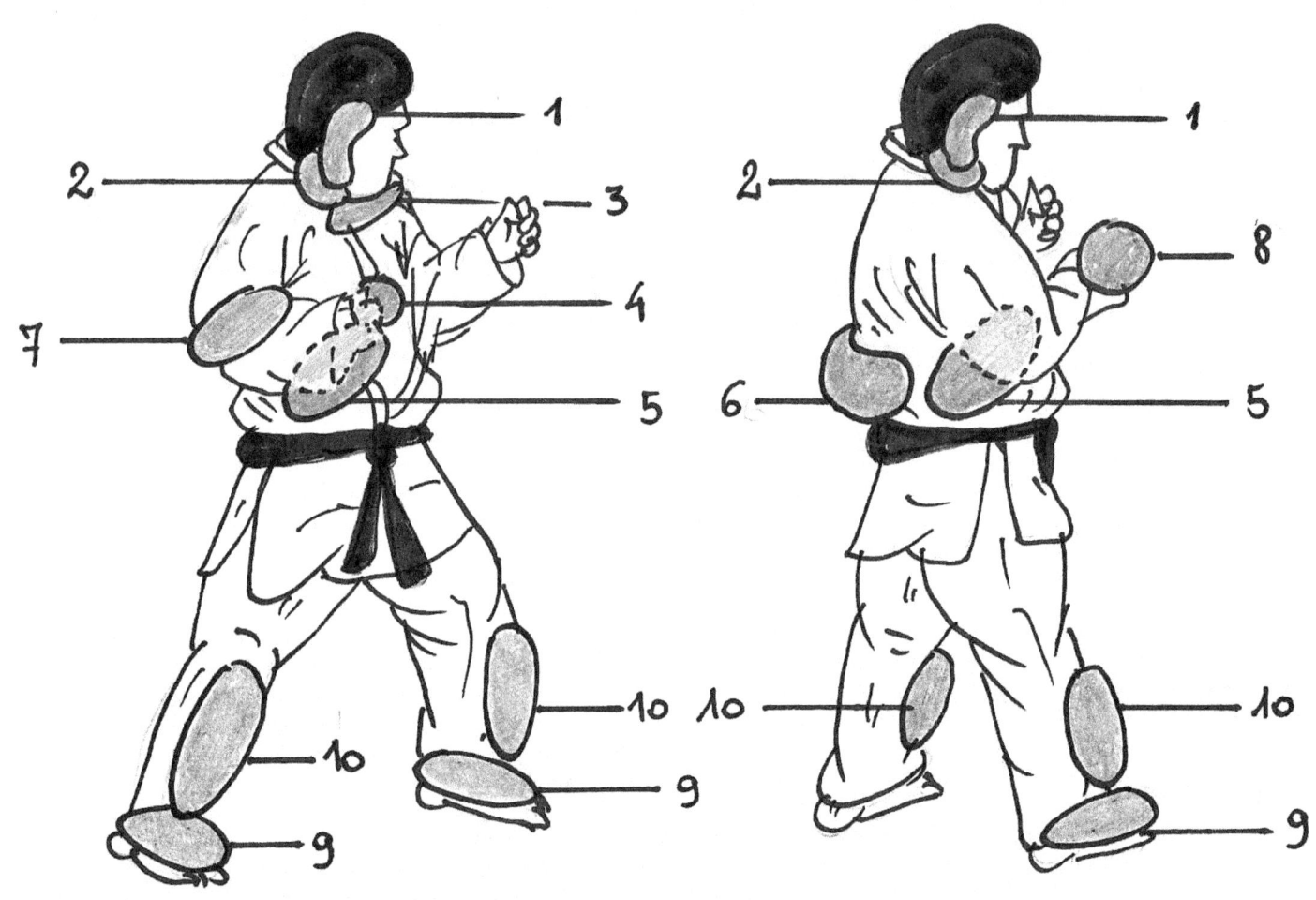

The Tertiary Targets of Krav Maga

Palm Strike to the face area: nose crush and fingers near the eyes

PART 3

Applied Krav Maga Series

טכניקות קרב מגע להגנה עצמית

1. General

Here follow no-nonsense applications of *Krav Maga* for self-defense that include the Kicks we have briefly presented. This will be what in Yiddish-derived Hebrew slang is called "**Tachles**" (טאכלעס): straight to the point, no circumlocutions, no unnecessary flowery additions,…
The Kicks will be part of the combinations, but only where needed. A *Krav Maga* practitioner does not kick just because he can; he kicks only if it is the most appropriate thing to do. So they can appear at the beginning, in the middle or at the end of the series. Or not at all…

Please do remember that *Krav Maga* is about survival in real world violence. The techniques presented are potentially debilitating or even lethal. They are to be drilled carefully and used only if there is no alternative. These techniques are not to be taught to children or teen-agers; only when sufficient maturity is reached can one really understand the consequences of one's actions.

The reader should practice the applied examples as they are. After serious drilling, the reader is invited to practice them with a partner that will resist a little. A technique is very easy on a cooperating partner 'just standing there'. Your partner should gradually 'resist' more in order to make your life more difficult, but also make your training more realistic. At this stage, your drills are just one notch below free-fighting. And then you'll see that sometimes your body takes over and that you unconsciously change the combination drilled to adapt it to your morphology and affinities. This is good and certainly the way to go. Keep training that way.
The day that you will have to really defend yourself against an aggression, your body will have to react *instinctively* and you will not have time to think. That's why you should drill all series presented, and then gradually focus on the ones that come to you naturally. To paraphrase, <u>*you certainly do not need to know the famous 10,000 techniques, but you should definitely drill the few ones that suit you for more than 10,000 times.*</u>

This training focus is even more important for the offensive techniques with which you can preempt an attack, if needed. After trying and seriously drilling dozens of such possible attacks, you should choose *only the 3 most suitable ones and drill them like crazy*. Drill only those ones, for power, penetration, stealth, precision, full commitment. Drill them again and again until they can become automatic and unstoppable. Then drill them more. They'll be there for you when and if the time comes…

I had a student who trained in Martial arts only for the self-defense aspect. To be ready, just in case... When proficient, he started to concentrate on *one* offensive technique only. He was drilling it all the time. It was simply a Jab/Cross pulling the rear leg for a 'Low Kick' to the knee. He learned to be very powerful with it, always kicking through with everything he had. He got used to make the kick very stealthy with the use of the hands. He drilled this offensive combination as a 'defensive' move: strike forward in the middle of the opponent's attack instead of blocking and retreating. And when the day came, this simple maneuver protected him from serious harm, getting rid of two aggressors in just twice " 1/2/3 ".

Learn, practice, drill and then start to *focus*.

Good Luck!

2. OFFENSIVE SERIES

Preemption is always better than defending and countering. And **Stop-striking** is second-best. The earlier you hit an assailant the better. Not only are these early techniques more effective, they also psychologically impress on your opponent that you are not a 'victim'. The reader is invited to refer to our book about 'Stop Kicks' for more general theories and techniques.

In the spirit of Israel's 6 Days War (1967), always take the initiative at the moment it becomes clear that a confrontation is inevitable. Once you understand that the fight cannot be avoided, or at the very moment you 'sense' that your opponent is about to launch (or just starts launching) his attack: go forward, strike and do not stop before he is vanquished. To an outside observer, it may seem that you are the attacker; but you are not, and better that than to be a victim... Just like in the Six Days War, you should aim at immediately neutralizing the fighting ability of your aggressor: destroy the limbs he needs to move and to strike.

The examples provided should be drilled as is; only when acquired and mastered, should you adapt them to your own affinities, but while respecting the **Krav Maga Principles** presented in the Introduction.

Our first example will underline the importance of always using your surroundings or anything that can help in a self-defense situation. See Illustrations at the top of next page. In this case, when confronted, you take the initiative by throwing anything you have towards the eyes of the opponent before he can attack you. Anything goes, especially if it is unexpected: your keys, small change from your pocket, a bag, a magazine, dirt or sand, a beverage,... Anything that will make him blink and lift his hands. You immediately follow with a *Front Kick to his groin*. Kick powerfully and *into* the target, *with full commitment and forward momentum*.. Lower your foot back and let it rebound on the floor for another powerful Front Kick, this time towards his *throat*, as he bends over in pain and lowers his hands towards his groin. Aim for the throat, but if you miss you'll still get the face. Deliver a Palm Strike to keep him busy as you lower your foot; strike through his hands if necessary to crush his *nose*. As he retreats or stumble backwards, aim a powerful Low Kick through his *knee* with precision (not the thigh but the knee joint). As you find yourself on his outward blind side, you can now stomp kick the back of his *knee* to make him unable to pursue you. Stomp through his knee, all the way to the ground.

Throw suddenly something towards his eyes to cover the start of your Groin Kick

If the potential assailant stands in a side guard or in opposite guard to yours, you can replace the Front Groin Kick by a *rear-leg Roundhouse Kick*, as illustrated in the next Figures. Aim precisely for the *groin* area and start your 'Retzev'. Attack the side of his neck to allow the safe lowering of your kicking leg. Grab his shoulder as he bends over from the pain, and punch the side of his head. Aim for the ear, and if you miss, you can still get the temple or the jaw hinge. Catch his head for a Knee Strike to the nose, but keep his head down for a Hammer-fist strike to the back of his neck, followed by another Groin Kick, this time Upward Front kick that can connect with the foot, the ankle or the chin according to the relative distance.

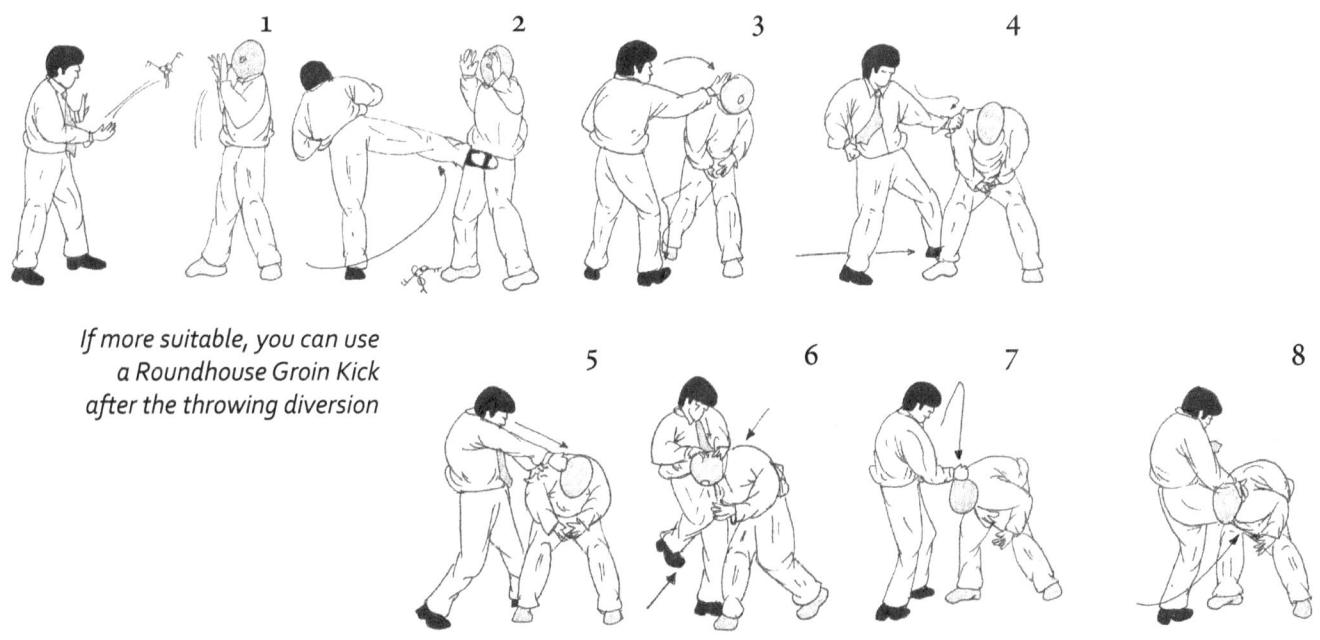

If more suitable, you can use a Roundhouse Groin Kick after the throwing diversion

OFFENSIVE SERIES

In the coming example, we illustrate an aggressive 'diving' towards the opponent, preferably just as he starts moving towards you to attack: he has not committed enough to be dangerous, but he is committed enough to be unable to change his momentum and his range calculations. That is ideal. By jumping forward, you completely foil his expectations and take the initiative. Remember that *Krav Maga* principles require you to be aggressive and offensive whenever possible. The Illustrations show clearly how you dive towards the assaillant, while extending your hands towards his face, in a way that protects your head. Aim at <u>poking your thumbs into his eyes,</u> and smoothly catch his head (or ears). With the same momentum, you *head-butt him on the nose* (with your upper forehead, where the hair scalp starts). After the head-butt, pull his neck down and kick his groin with your rear leg, preferably with the upper ankle. Remember to kick up & through a few inches above the target. Let your kicking foot rebound on the floor for a powerful Knee Strike to his face, and then rebound again for a second Knee Strike to his groin. The reader notices easily the alternation of sensitive targets at different levels: *Retzev* at its best! You lower the kneeing leg while already pivoting into a dangerous *Head Twist Takedown*: you simply twist his head with both hands towards the ground in the deepest possible circular move [**Be extremely gentle and controlled in training, this is a potentially crippling technique!**]. Once he is on the ground, you can further neutralize him by stomping his elbow, his ankle or his fingers.

Dive in a protected way towards the attacker's eyes, and start to follow-up uninterruptedly

KRAV MAGA KICKS

The next set of Drawings illustrates another way to 'dive' towards an assailant about to attack; a way that is particularly good against opponents with a high closed guard. You suddenly jump forward *while trying to catch the opponent's wrists*, or at least to block any possible movement of his hands towards you. It is much easier than it seems, as you take the initiative unexpectedly when the opponent is just about to attack. You can then strike the *side of his head* with a circular *Elbow Strike* (use the hips), while letting go of one of his wrists very late in the strike. Pivot back with your hips while bringing back your arm in a Hammer-fist Strike to the other side of his head. Lift your front foot in a Front Ghost Groin Kick, kicking up a few inches into the testicles. While lowering your foot, you deliver a Palm Strike to his nose; if possible and adequate, let your fingers touch his eyes to overwhelm him. The striking hands goes then to catch the back of his neck as you knee his groin with a powerful rear-leg move. As he reels back, simply extend the leg into an Upward Groin Kick with the foot or the shin. Now is the time to bring him down with a Stomping Kick to the side of his knee, while you pull him down in a twist: pull on his arm and push violently on his head. As you should have kept hold of his arm all the way, you could pull his extended elbow sharply to your shin to cause joint damage (Keep control of his body while doing that). You can finish him up, for example with a downward Elbow Strike to the head.

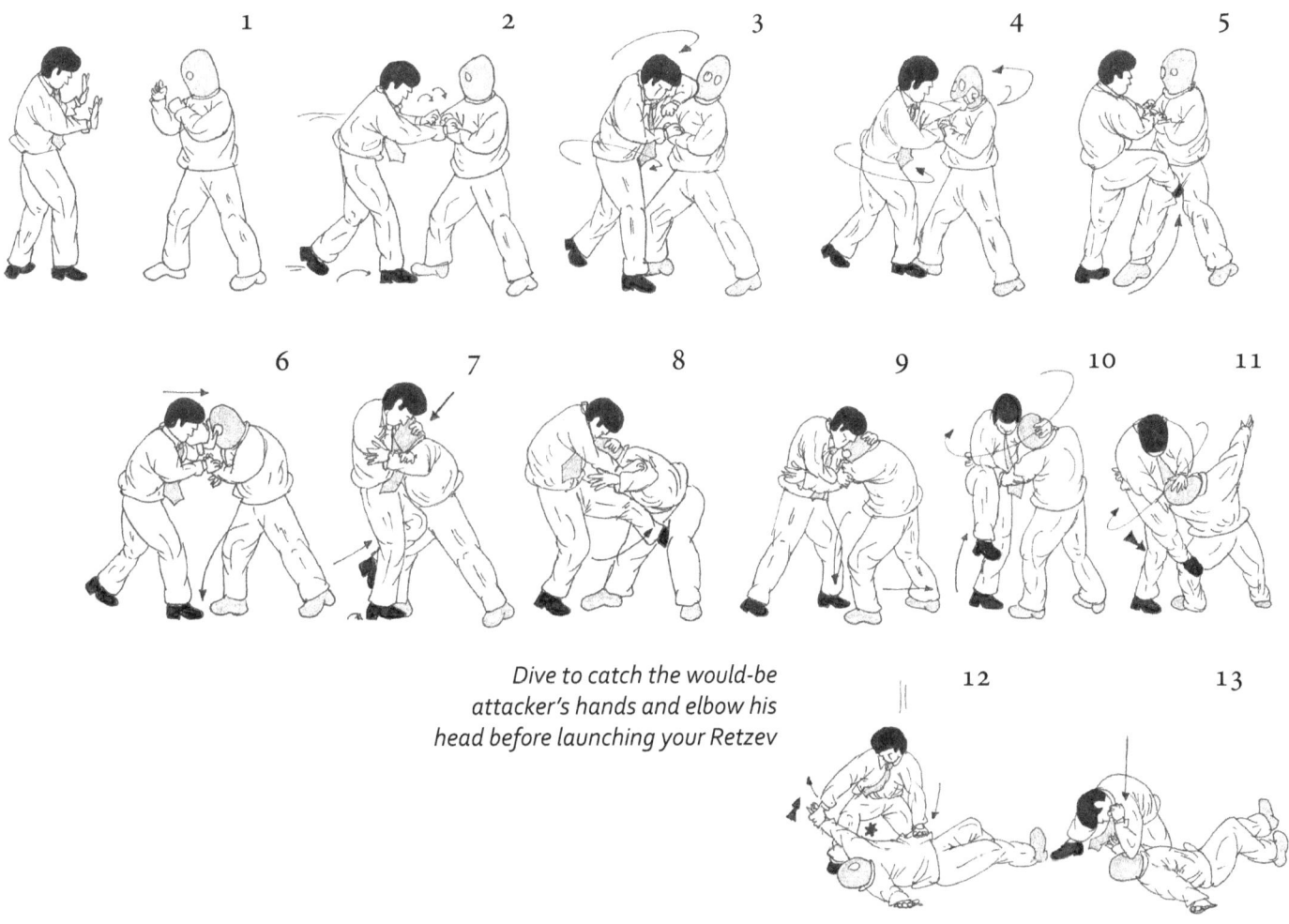

Dive to catch the would-be attacker's hands and elbow his head before launching your Retzev

OFFENSIVE SERIES

Another very useful opening is **the Finger Whip**. This is a very simple and easy maneuver well worth drilling for its speed and effectiveness. You simply throw your relaxed fingers into the *eyes* of the assailant, You do not try to poke, but just whip (like with a towel) to 'crack' in the eyes area. This is an extremely fast strike, because the whole arm is completely relaxed: you do not need strength and precision like for a punch or a poke. You simply extend fast towards the eyes and pull back even faster. The fingers strike the eyes while passing in front, and the fast pulling-back create a powerful whipping undulation. This is very close in execution to the classic Backfist Strike of traditional Martial Arts (*Uraken Uchi* in *Karatedo*). In any case, nobody can prevent reacting to a fast strike towards the eyes.

While you retract your whipping arm, you deliver a Low Front Kick (Regular or 'Soccer') to the opponent's front *knee*. Chamber back and switch smoothly to a stomping Low Side Kick to the same knee. Kick 'into' the knee, not on its surface. Do not chamber back, but go down with the foot to stomp his ankle and the top of his foot. Crush his foot as if trying to obliterate it into the floor. Try to keep control of his front arm for additional safety (You can also Palm-strike his nose to keep him off-balance). Move your crushing foot out and strike with a Circular Elbow powered by the hips; aim for the ear (side of the face). Follow-up with a naturally-flowing Knee to the groin. Your opponent is already hurt, so you can lower the foot and pull back your front foot to gather momentum for an 'all-out' Low Kick through the knee. Of course, your own 'Retzev' could look different, once you have acquired some experience and let your own personality drive your follow-ups.

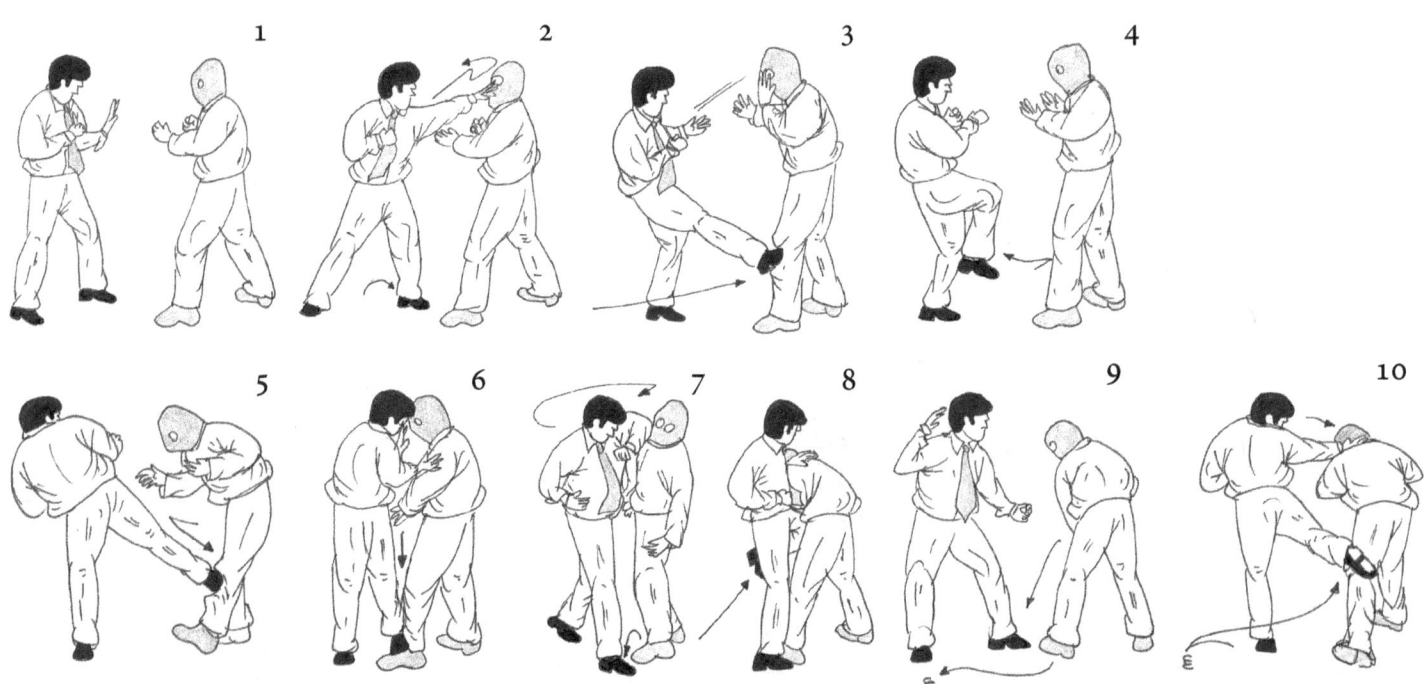

Open with an ultra-fast Finger Whip and a Low Front Kick, then start your Retzev

The coming Illustrations will show another way to use the all-important **Finger Whip**: attack **low** first as a painful diversion, *then* rake his eyes. The *Front Low Kick* is a very fast, effective and stealthy kick, as described at length in our previous books 'Low Kicks' and 'Stealth Kicks'. Just make sure you keep your upper body as still as possible while executing the Kick. Aim for the *knee*, preferably just below it, and kick a few inches *into* the target before retracting the leg. While retracting the kicking foot, whip towards his eyes while his attention is down. Immediately, use your front leg to fast Roundhouse-kick his groin, hopping forward if necessary. This is a fast combination executed with relaxed muscles and that is well-worth drilling a lot to make it natural. Now that your opponent has been kicked in the testicles, you can start your *Retzev*. Suggested here is: a rear-leg fully-powered Roundhouse Kick to the kidneys (Lower Back), a hip-powered Palm Strike to the nose as you lower the kicking leg, a Knee Strike to the groin (again) and then, a throat-holding Takedown of your flustered opponent. For that, you strike his throat with the part of the hand between your thumb and your forefinger, and then you grip his Adam's apple. Keep control of his arm, place your rear leg behind his front one as if for an Outer Reap Throw and twist him down in a spiral over this leg. Make sure you keep the Throat Squeeze and use your whole body to twist him down. Bang his head on the floor, and stomp his armpit to neutralize his arm.

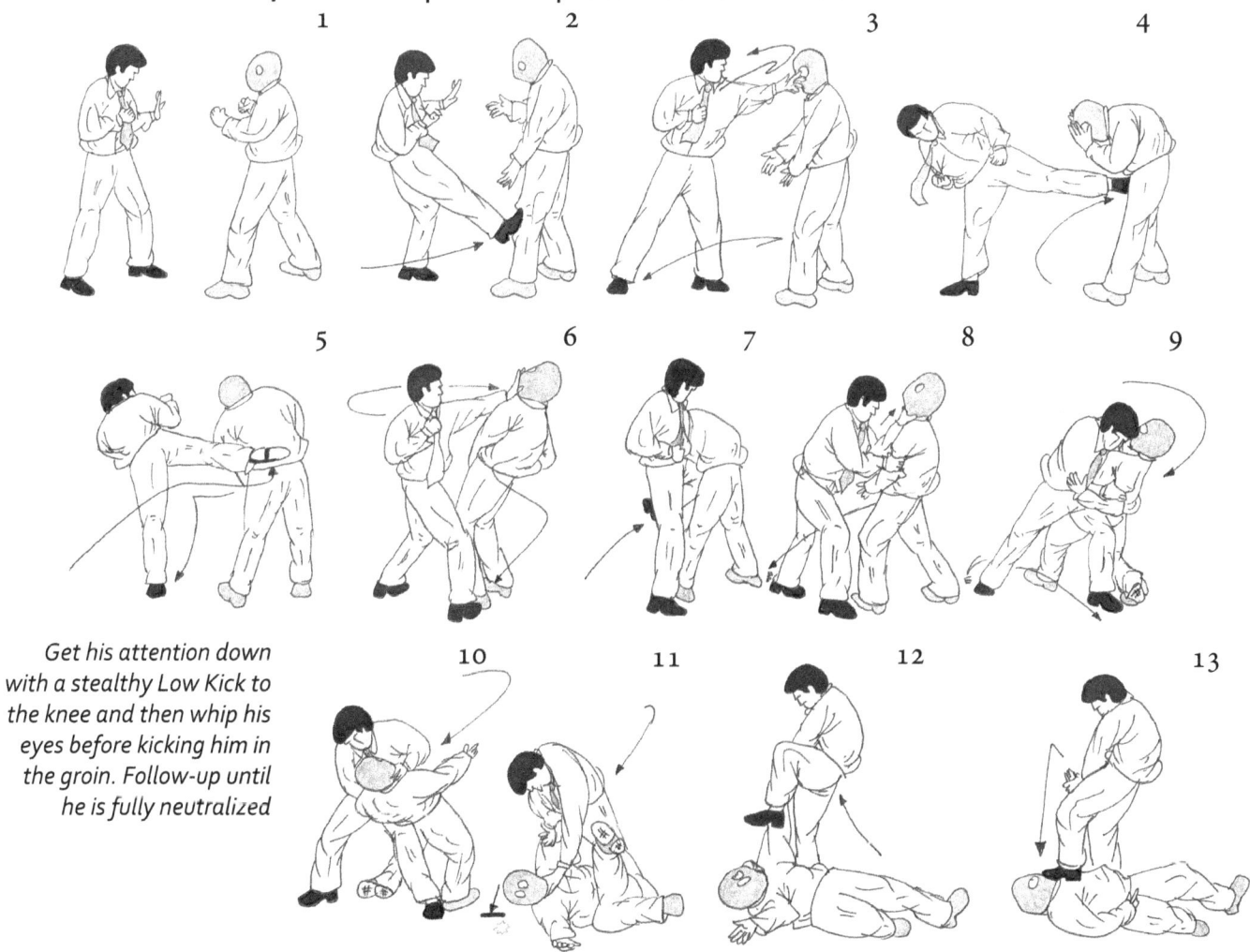

Get his attention down with a stealthy Low Kick to the knee and then whip his eyes before kicking him in the groin. Follow-up until he is fully neutralized

OFFENSIVE SERIES

There are many techniques that can be used for a pre-emptive attack, and we cannot present them all.

We shall close this Chapter with a last opening: a **Stealth Hopping Small Roundhouse Kick to the groin**. It is important to keep the upper body immobile for as long as possible, and hop towards the opponent as late as possible in the execution. The maneuver is best used when the potential assailant is far enough from you to feel secure. You will lift your hand up to draw his attention while you lift your front leg to start a Small Roundhouse. It is only after the foot is on its way that you will hop towards the opponent, just enough to reach his groin. Bend slightly rearwards to avoid a possible Stop Punch. Once the opponent bends over in pain, follow up: a Hammer-fist Strike to the back or the side of his neck and a powerful Low Kick through the side of his knee. You can now 'own' his back for the finish: an Upwards Groin Kick from behind, followed by a Stomp Kick to crush his knee into the ground. If the altercation is very serious, you can conclude with a Knife-hand Strike to his throat that you can expose by pulling his head back. In more civilized settings, you can simply hammer-fist his nose and leave it at that....

A surprising opening against an opponent standing out of punching range: the Stealth Hopping Roundhouse Groin Kick

3. DEFENSES AGAINST PUNCHES

There are all kinds of punching attacks and all kinds of ways to cope with them. Of course, the best course of action is always to preempt the attack as soon as you discern that the confrontation is inevitable. Of course, it is not always possible and we will examine three broad categories of Punching Attacks: the Haywire Punching from far away, the Punching Flurry and the more traditional 'regular' Punching.

The reader is invited to note that, from this point on, the book will present shorter examples of *Retzev* in the Applications. The principles of 'Retzev' have been made very clear by the previous examples and the reader will easily develop his own preferences according to his affinities and psychology. We will still scatter a few longer examples here and there for completeness, but it is the basic defense technique that will be underlined from now on. This does not mean that the 'Retzev' follow-up is not necessary: not at all! **Retzev** importance has been made clear but is now left to the reader.

3.1 The Haywire Punch

Haywire Punching is the wide range punches from out of range with the opponent rushing you. You can see the attack from far away, but it is still a very dangerous situation, because the attack comes with lots of energy from the momentum and the wide trajectory. If you get struck, it is a serious blow and probably the start of a series of subsequent punches.

The best approach against such an attack is **Stop-kicking**. In the first example, presented at the top of next page, you are a bit surprised by the sudden launch of the rushing punch and you slightly retreat to allow for a *Front Stop Kick* to the attacker's *groin*. Lean rearwards while kicking to keep out of trouble. Kick forcefully up *into* the groin. Remember that you have to stop the assailant in his tracks and that a surface strike will not suffice. As he stops and steps back in pain, you can follow-up with a Knee Strike to the nose and a low Kick to the knee that will make him pivot and present his back. A powerful Penetrating Front Kick to his kidneys (lower back) could be the start of your own Retzev, but everything else goes.

For a Haywire Punch you see coming, lean back and stop it with a Front Groin Kick; follow-up, for example, with Knee Strike (face), Low Kick (knee) and Front Kick (kidneys)

Another way to follow up on the *Groin Stop Kick* would be to catch his head to place it in position for a powerful *Knife-hand Strike to the back of his neck*, as illustrated in the following Photos.

After the Groin Stop Kick, you could start your 'Retzev' with a Downward Strike to the Cervical Vertebrae

Of course, the Stop Kick could easily be a **Side Stop Kick** to the *knee* that will stop his forward movement. Remember to kick forcefully *through* the knee to inflict damage. You can follow up with a rebounding Side Kick to his Floating Ribs, and then a Hammer-fist or a Back-fist Strike to the side of his head (Temple, ear, or mandibular joint). This will get his attention up and open his groin for a fast Roundhouse. Keep at it!

A Side Stop Kick to the knee will also deal with a rushing punch; let the leg rebound for a repeat Side kick to the floating ribs

Of course, a regular **Block & Counter** is always a possibility for such a clear attack. Go forward towards it and remember that *blocking* means: 'striking the incoming limb with force in order to cause it damage'. Block the incoming wide Hook Punch by striking the arm with your Forearm or Knife-hand. Immediately (**nearly simultaneously**!) follow up with a crippling Counter like those illustrated in the Photos below, and of course, add your own 'Retzev'.

Block forcefully and simultaneously strike the opponent's eyes or throat

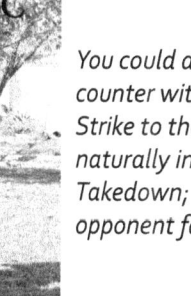

You could also block and then counter with an Upward Palm Strike to the chin that flows naturally into an Outer Reap Takedown; makes sure the opponent falls on his head

DEFENSES AGAINST PUNCHES

3.2 The Punching Flurry

The **Punching Flurry** is much more difficult to deal with, especially if you have been taken by surprise. The assailant is close and throws short punches in series, none fully committed, but all dangerous. As soon as he will score 'a good one', the attacker will start his own *Retzev*. This is the typical careful *Jab/Cross/Jab* approach of the trained boxer. *Blocking is of no use* as the punching arm is immediately retracted while the other one is already on its way.
There are 2 basic ways to deal with the Punching Flurry: <u>*Evade*</u> or <u>*Jam*</u>. **Evading** is not to be where his punches are directed by going down, rearwards, sideways or any combination of those. **Jamming** is protecting yourself while proactively diving towards his punches for a close-combat aggressive series. A few examples will make all this clear.

The more '*Krav Maga*' option is always the aggressive assault one. So, when attacked with a flurry of punches to the head, you protect yourself tightly with your elbows as illustrated. And you immediately <u>dive</u> forward *towards* the opponent, which he will not expect. It is possible that you will be hit on the way, but not only are you protected enough to absorb some of it, but all the range calculations and the expectations of your opponent are foiled. You are effectively jamming his attacks and you are scoring a serious psychological blow: you are not retreating like an easy prey, but you are on the contrary attacking with no fear. Once in range, catch his head and use your forward momentum for a *Head Butt* to the center of his face (*nose*). The movement will then flow naturally, nearly automatically, into a Groin Knee Strike, followed by an Elbow Strike to the side of the head or the side of the neck. A great follow-up from this position goes through another Groin Strike, with the shin this time, while you get hold of his chin from above and around. You'll have then to proceed <u>slowly and carefully in training</u> for a *Chin Twist Takedown*. Twist him by the chin (and shoulder) to take him down to the ground and try to slam his head into the ground. **<u>Be very careful, as a brusque Chin Twist is extremely dangerous and potentially lethal</u>**. Let the circumstances dictate your behavior.
The series is illustrated at the top of next page.

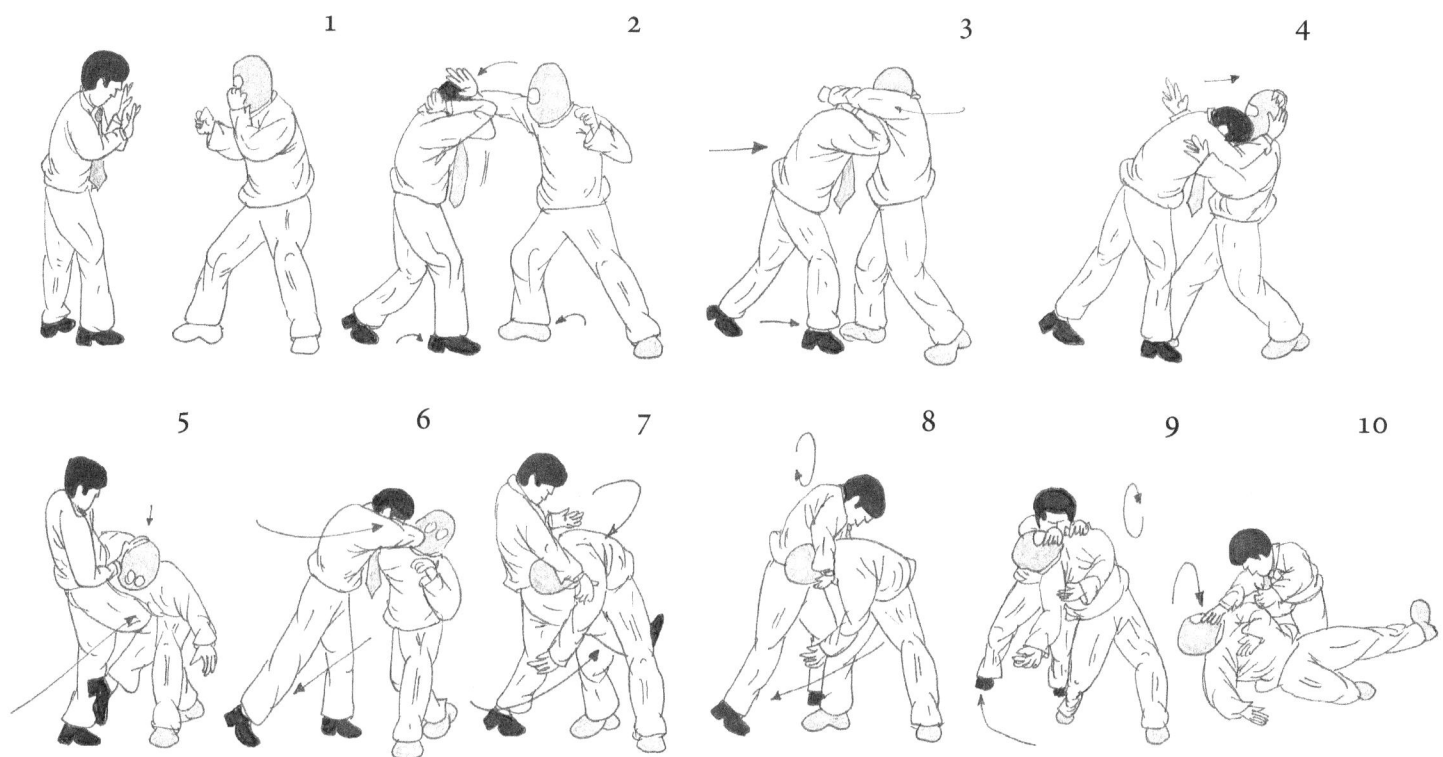

Protect your head by forming a 'helmet' with your arms and dive in

The other possibility is to **evade and counter**. If you are surprised by a sudden rush with a flurry of Punches, the best way is probably to slightly retreat and bend the trunk away from the Punch. The good side of it, is that it places you in ideal position for a simultaneous 'Body-bent' or 'Hand-on-floor' Kick.

The next Figures, at the top of next page, illustrate how you retreat, bend and simultaneously kick the assailant's forward knee. Once he is stopped, let your kicking foot rebound on the floor to attack his floating ribs or groin area with another *Body-bent Side Kick*. Of course, you need to keep the initiative. You could whip towards his eyes as you straighten up, and crush his face with a hip-powered Palm Strike. As his attention is now definitely up, you can now execute an Outward Ghost Groin Kick with all your body in it. Finish by coming back with a Lateral Elbow Strike to his neck.

Evade back while executing a Hand-on-floor Stop Kick

The other way to evade a punching combination is **by going down**, under the punches. Punching flurries usually attack the head; if you go down on one knee (while still guarding your head), you will surprise the assailant who is launched to punch in the air above you. The effect of <u>surprise</u> is, all other parameters constant, a great equalizer. The motto of the *Mossad*, the much respected Israeli Secret Service, is in Biblical Hebrew something like :

"By way of deception, thou shalt make war" (בתחבולות תעשה לך מלחמה).
That is what we shall be doing here. It is true that such a move is not without danger, but its brazenness and unexpectedness, make it a very effective move. The reader is invited to consult our book about 'Stealth Kicks' and to remember that surprising tactics are to be used parsimoniously, lest they lose their effect.

In our example illustrated at the top of next page, you go down on one knee, <u>under</u> the *Jab/Cross* combination rushing your way. You simultaneously punch your assailant's *groin* with your own Jab/Cross. Strike forcefully and penetrate into the target to send a shock wave through the area. Stand up with an Uppercut to the throat (or chin if you miss) and finish the opponent with a Stealth Groin Kick and a Knee Strike to the nose as he bends in pain. You could continue with another Groin Kick (Regular Upward Front Kick) if necessary, but it should have been enough.

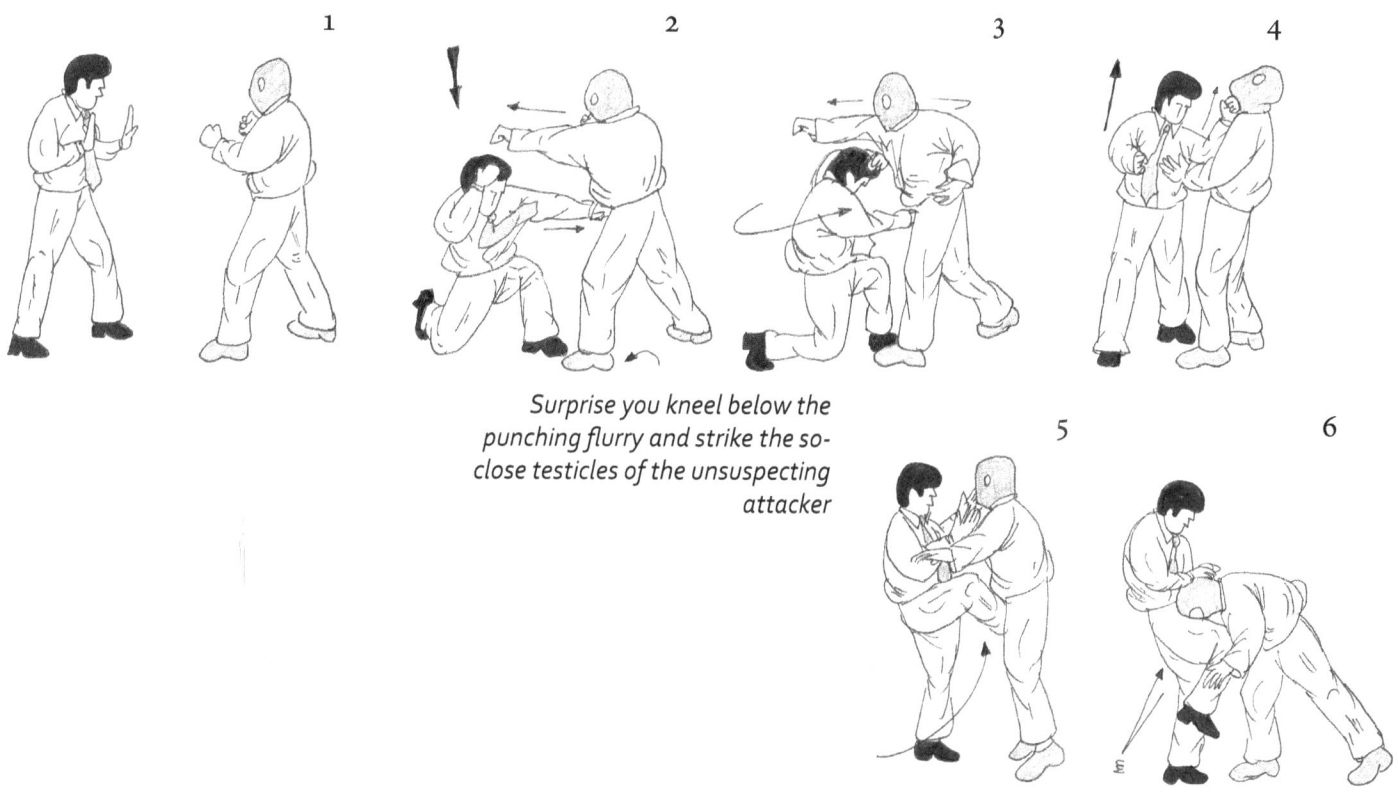

Surprise you kneel below the punching flurry and strike the so-close testicles of the unsuspecting attacker

3.3 More traditional Punches

This section will deal briefly with the more traditional punches and with the classic way to handle them. *Krav Maga* will always favor the *Stop Kick* or the *Stop Punch* when dealing with a striking attack. Only when there is no choice, will the Artist use the classic 'Block and Counter' *with the mindset of starting the counter as early as possible*. The coming Photos (next page) illustrate the most appropriate Stop Kicks against regular straight punches from normal range: <u>Small Roundhouse to the groin and Side Kick to the floating ribs</u>. Obviously, a kick to the groin will stop a punch in mid-trajectory. And the same happen if you side-kick the ribs that are 'opened' by the execution of the Punch itself. Stop-kicking requires some bending back in order to place the head just out of reach of the punch; it is very natural and even helps the delivery of the Kick.

What is left after one of these Stop Kicks is to start your own *Retzev*; I have found that a *"same-leg Stomping Side Kick to the back of the knee"* is a good follow-up to be built upon.

Stealthy Groin Roundhouse against a Jab

Stealthy Groin roundhouse against a Cross

Side Kick to the floating ribs opened up by the opponent's jab itself

Side Kick to the floating ribs against a Cross

KRAV MAGA KICKS

Same Side stop Kick against a Cross punch in opposite stances

Stop Punches are the next best approach; but they will require some angling out and some control of the incoming punch, *unlike Stop Kicks that usually will require simple bending back out of range*. The most effective approach is the simultaneous '**Block & Punch**'; it requires training and the mindset of going forward into an attack, but it is surprisingly easy to perform.

Our first example in the Figures below illustrates how to tackle a *Jab* attack with an *Outside 'Block' and a simultaneous Inside Jab*. The principle is pretty simple, but it requires drilling for proficiency. The technique is very naturally followed by a front-leg Groin Roundhouse Kick and a subsequent 'Low Kick' to the opponent's front knee.

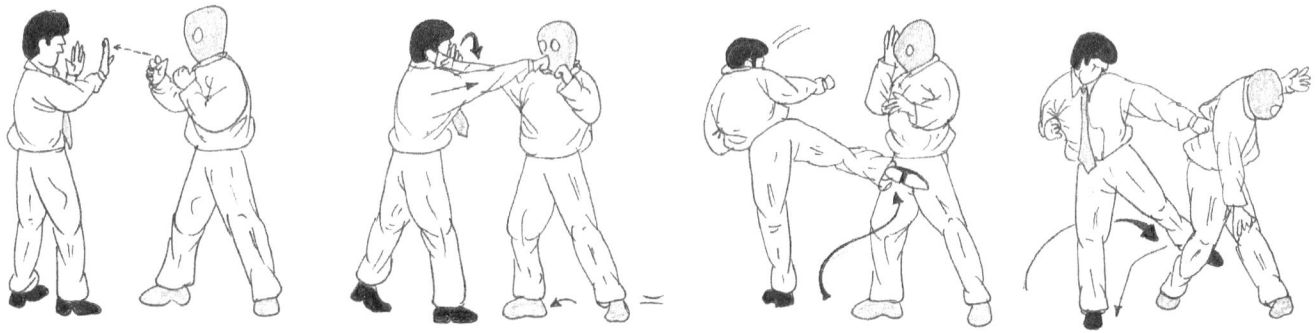

Simultaneous 'Parry & Punch' against a Jab, and follow-up

Of course, the same technique is applicable to dealing with a *Cross Punch*. The second set of Drawings, at the top of next page, shows how it is done and followed by a different *Retzev*: Front Groin Kick, Palm Strike to the nose, Knee strike to the floating ribs, and Downward Elbow Strike to the back of the neck.

DEFENSES AGAINST PUNCHES

Simultaneous 'Parry & Punch' against a Cross Punch, and follow-up

A last example of *simultaneous 'Block & Punch'* is presented in the following Illustrations. The Block is a classic 'Enveloping Downward Block' that takes the incoming *Jab* 'down and out' from above. The simultaneous Strike is a front hand Palm attack to his nose, with your fingertips in the general area of his eyes. You could follow then with a fast front-leg Groin Roundhouse Kick.

Downward Block of a Jab with a simultaneous front-hand Palm Strike

Sometimes, a simultaneous 'Block and Counter' is not possible, and the best next option is a **<u>Block that turns into a Strike</u>**. Remember that, in *Krav Maga*, it is important to regain the initiative as fast and as early as possible. In the first example (illustrated at the top of next page), you parry a *Cross* from the outside and then extend your arm over his (pressing it down and in) to become a Punch to his face. While doing this, you use your hips to power the Punch and to take you out of the center-line. Start your own *Retzev* from here.

120   KRAV MAGA KICKS

Outside Block of a Cross becomes a Punch to the face

Another example follows and presents an *Upward Parry turning into a Punch*. In this technique, you duck below a Cross Punch while parrying upwards with your front hand. Your arm then extends naturally towards his throat (or chin) slightly from below. The proposed start of the follow-up is an Upward Front Kick to the groin, as illustrated below.

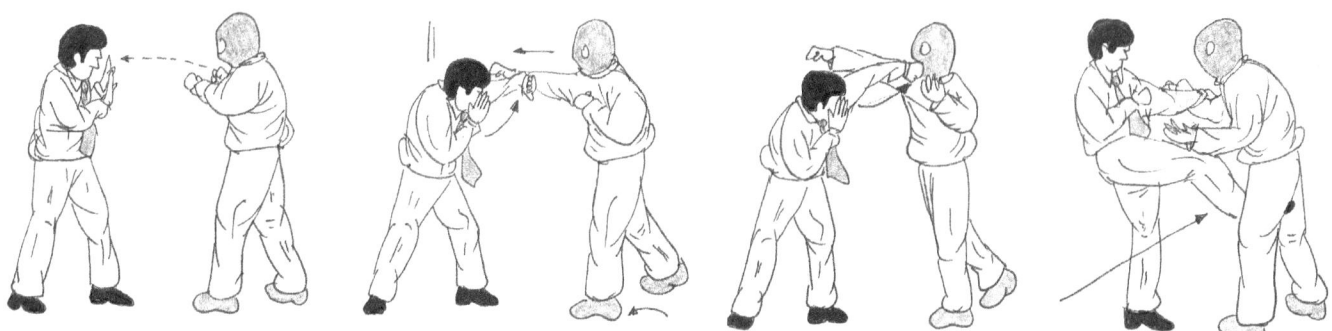

Upward Parry of a Cross becomes a Strike to the throat

And now, the next set of Drawings illustrates the classic *Inside Knife-hand Block turning naturally into a Knife-hand or Forearm Strike to the throat* or the side of the neck. Our example is against a Jab and is followed by a fast front-leg Groin Roundhouse kick. Take it from there…

Inside Block of a Jab becomes a Strike to the neck

DEFENSES AGAINST PUNCHES

Of course, sometimes, these quasi-simultaneous techniques are not possible. You just have time to block and use the other hand to keep covered. The idea is now **to counter as fast and as early as possible**. It will be a classic '<u>**Block and Counter**</u>', but the *Krav Maga* philosophy is (1) to go on the offensive as fast as possible (even if it endangers you a little), (2) to counter towards the most sensitive targets possible, and (3) to keep hitting without hiatus. In our example below, you go towards the Hook Punch to block it and keep this forward-and-out momentum to strike the attacker's throat with the forearm of the other (rear) arm. Keep control of his arm while following up by kneeing his groin and headbutting his face. You can then use his arm to pull him around and get his back. Set a Rear Choke while strengthening your control, preferably with your fingers in his eyes.

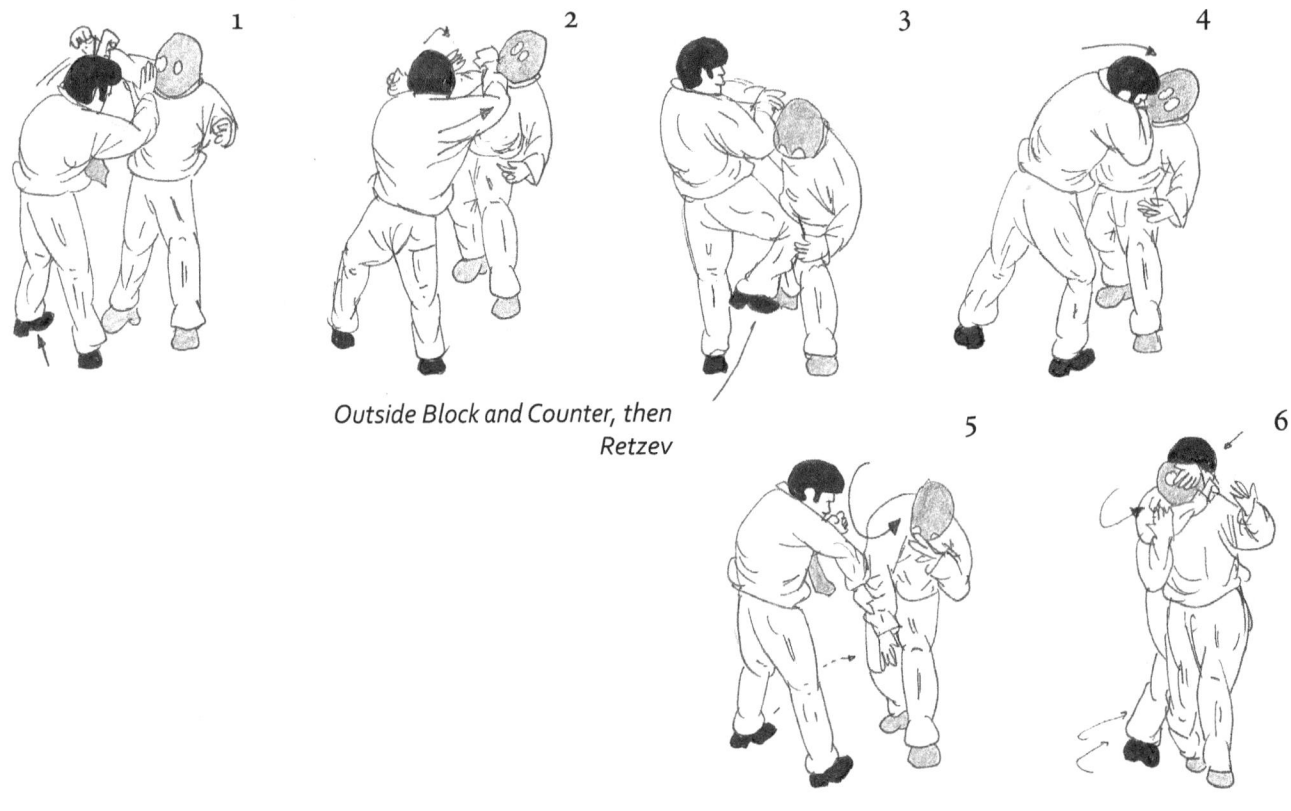

Outside Block and Counter, then Retzev

A lifetime of training for just ten seconds.
~Jesse Owens

4. DEFENSES AGAINST KICKS

<u>Kicks</u> by relatively untrained assailants are usually easier to handle than punching attacks, as they come from further away, and they offer opportunities for fierce defenses and counters. The flip side of the coin is that kicking attacks by trained Martial Artists require a more careful approach.

We shall present the selected Krav Maga techniques categorized by the type of Kick, starting with the Front Kick, which is the most common with untrained attackers. Still, do not underestimate any assailant and remember that a kick usually targets your groin, the sensitive target *par excellence*.

4.1 Defenses against Front Kicks

A. <u>*The best way*</u> to handle a Front Kick is, of course, **preemptive**: assault the potential assailant just as he has taken the decision to kick. If you start early enough, any preemptive attack will do. If you are slightly late to the party, then the best approach is to go forward and stop-kick his own kicking leg, preferably with a fast Front Low Soccer Kick to the shin. You can then use your forward momentum for a close-up *Retzev*. Kicking the shin of a leg travelling towards you is very effective: it is psychologically disturbing, it foils all of the opponent's plans and distance calculations, and it adds the energy of *his* kick to the impact. If you are wearing hard-soled shoes, all the better.

Stop Kick to the shin of the opponent's kicking leg in development

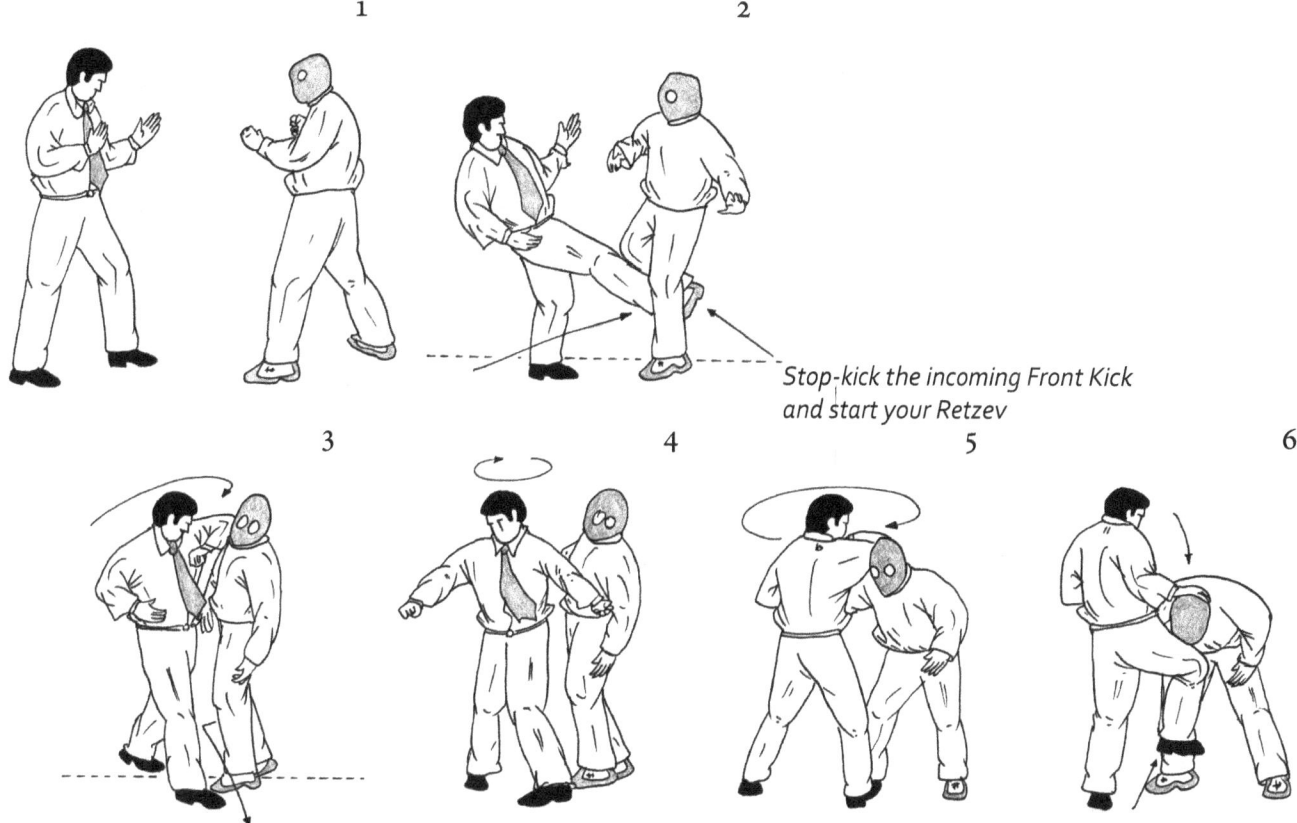

Stop-kick the incoming Front Kick and start your Retzev

The principle of kicking the shin of a developing Front Kick stays the same if you use a *Low Side Stop Kick*, as illustrated below.

Side Stop Kick to the shin of an incoming Front Kick

Of course, if you have the time and necessary speed, you could directly attack his groin as he starts his Front Kick. This is usually a front-leg Upward Front Groin Kick. This is not far-fetched at all, as you 'feel' his attack coming, and as your opponent counts on you staying in place (or retreating) and develops his kick accordingly.

Go for his testicles with your own Front Kick, as soon as you discern his attack

DEFENSES AGAINST KICKS

B. _The most elegant way_ to deal with a Front kick is **to evade and then counter fast**, preferably while the kick is still being executed. The best example is the Forward Diagonal Evasion with a Groin Kick while the attacker's leg is still in the air. The technique is very simple, extremely effective, but requires drilling and flawless timing!

Evade forward and out, and kick the attacker's 'open' groin"

The evading Stop Strike needs not be necessarily a Kick. In the Illustrations below, we show an evasion to the outside of the kicking leg, with a _simultaneous Punch to the face_ (chin or nose). The impact is very strong because of the forward momentum of the attacker. You can then kick his groin from behind, before his kicking foot lands and conclude with a Forearm Strike to the back of his exposed neck.

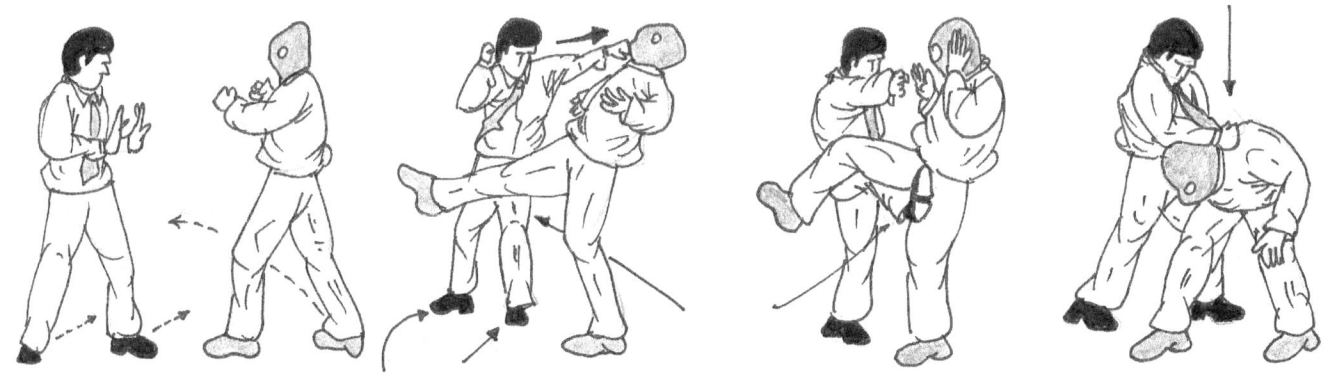

Evading Punch against a committed Front Kick attack, and follow-up

Of course, the evasion can also be _rearwards_, out of range. Such an evasion, is usually done with some form of control of the incoming kick. In the example illustrated by the Photos at the top of next page, you retreat just enough to keep out of range of the kick; and then, you attack the knee of the landing leg. Kick _through the knee, in a stomping movement_, and start your _Retzev_ (by starting with a high Strike).

Evade rearwards with some control of the attacking kick, and attack the landing knee with a powerful Low Front kick

C. *The defenses left to cover are the more classic* **'Block & Counter'**. Generally, the blocking is more of a 'deviating' maneuver that takes the momentum of the kick and takes it enough of course to neutralize the danger. To use your arms to block a kick head to head with brute force is not a very intelligent approach: the legs are much stronger and you will end up hurting your hands or forearms.

Our first example will be the 'blocking' version of the previous forward-evading technique with *Groin Kick*. In this case, you have evaded rearwards while blocking down outwards. You can scoop and grab the kicking ankle if you can; or you can just block and kick. If you have scooped the ankle you can also pull the leg forward to place the opponent slightly off-balance and keep him in the air longer. But the simple *Block and Kick* technique is certainly easier and effective enough. In the Photos below, we illustrate the scooping block, but with no pulling the attacker forward. As soon as the blocking deviation is achieved and you are out of danger, your Groin Kick is on its way.

Evade back with controlling block and kick the attacker's open groin

DEFENSES AGAINST KICKS

When you block a Front Kick and block with a lateral evasion, you can either evade to the *inside* of the kicking assailant, or to the *outside*. You block to inflect the course of the kick while going *diagonally forward* just enough to be outside of the direct vector of the kick development. In the spirit of *Krav Maga*, you should then start your counter as early as possible.

*Evade **outside** the kicking leg and counter with a Ridge-hand Throat Strike as he lands forward*

*Evade **inside** the kicking leg and start your Retzev with a Groin Strike and a Palm attack of his face*

*Another example of follow-up after an evasion block **outside** the kicking leg*

One of the most stunning technique against a Front Kick (and a Roundhouse) is the **Big Inner Reap Takedown**, coming for Ju Jitsu's *O Uchi Gari*. This Takedown can be executed after you have blocked and scooped the attacking leg, and it then becomes a *very stunning and dangerous maneuver*: done mildly it will at least stun your opponent and take his breath out; done by lifting him as high as possible and then pushing his head down first it can be lethal.

The first example below shows an evading-forward scooping Block to the inside of the kicking leg. Once you have grabbed the leg, knee the opponent's groin, poke or whip his eyes, and then grab him for the reaping Takedown. If the confrontation is serious push his head down as he falls. If it is not enough, note that you are holding his opened legs and that you can punch his groin fast before releasing them.

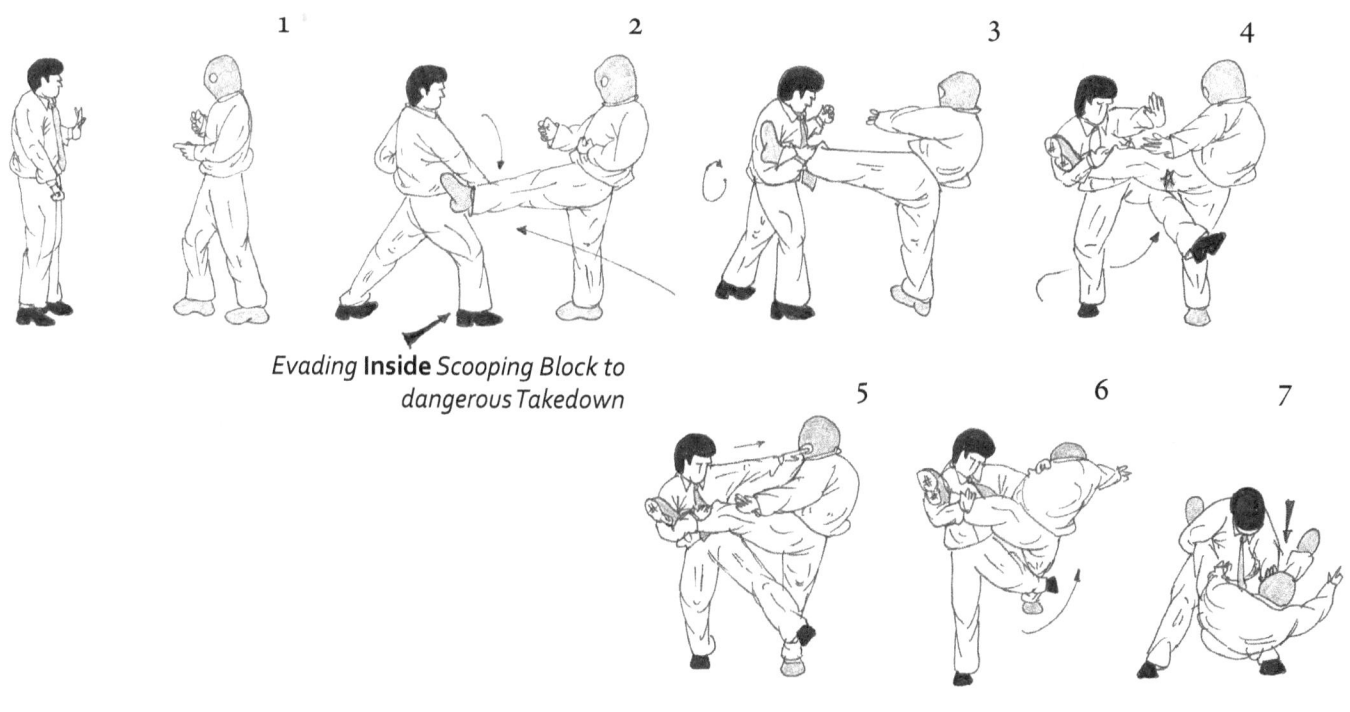

*Evading **Inside** Scooping Block to dangerous Takedown*

DEFENSES AGAINST KICKS

This coming second set of Drawings illustrates the same technique following an *Outside Scooping Block* of his Front Kick Attack. Once the leg grabbed and lifted, you whip or poke his eyes to get safely closer, then take hold of the back of his head. Palm-strike his face (your other hand keeps his head in place) and then push it down towards the floor while reaping off his standing leg. If he falls on his back, he will be seriously rattled, somewhat hurt and breathing with difficulty. If he falls on his head, he will be veryseriously hurt. Be careful and rational!

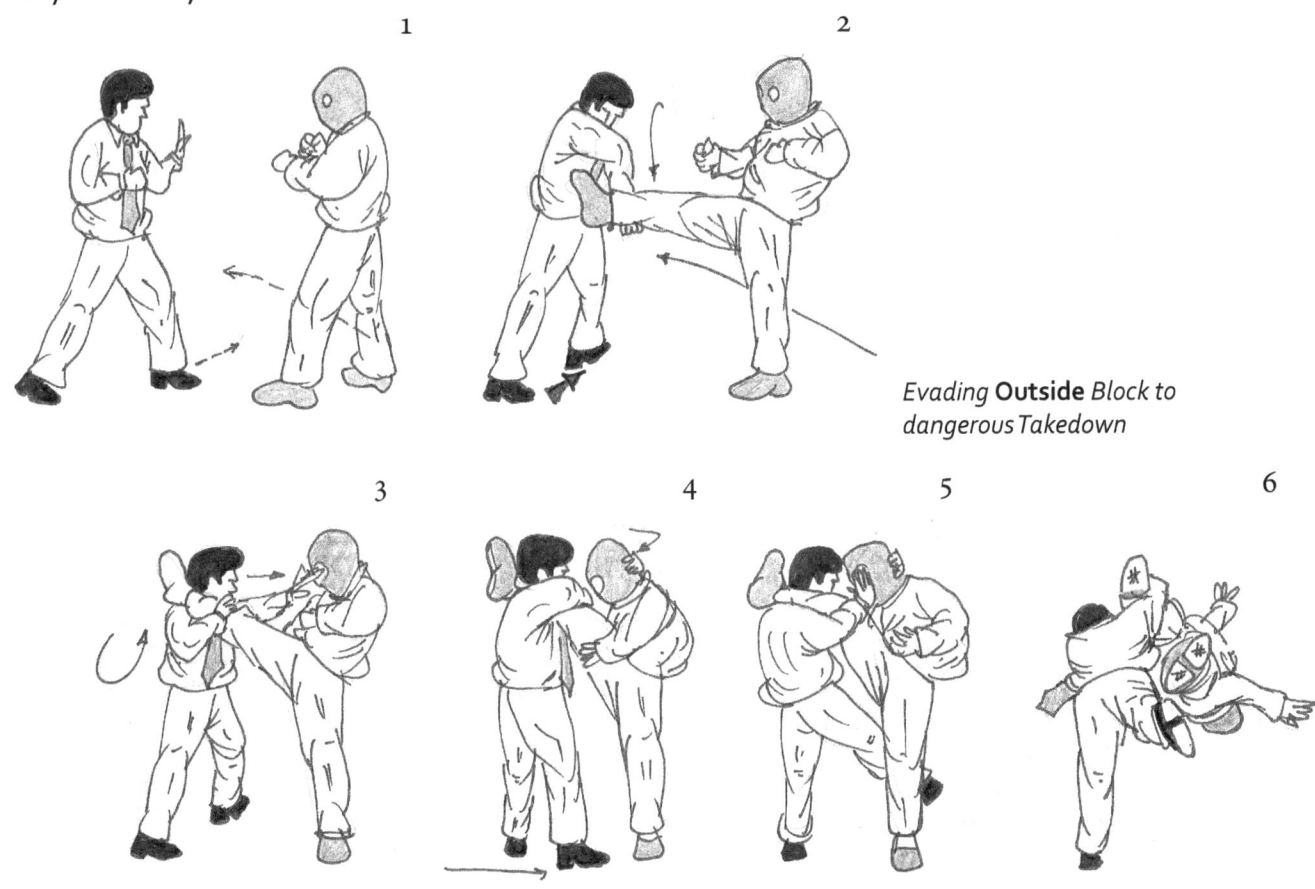

*Evading **Outside** Block to dangerous Takedown*

D. *The last general defense tactic to mention is the Leg Block.* Instead of deviating the kick with your hands, you will do so with your lower leg. The **Leg Block** is very simple, but it requires familiarization and some training to master it enough for intuitive use. But the important advantage of this kind of block is that you do not need to bend forward or to open your guard: you stay in guard and block, then counter. The Illustrations at the top of next page show how to slightly move out of the center-line, in order to leg-block the incoming Front Kick on the *outside*. Counter with a Palm Strike to the face as you lower the blocking leg. As your deviating block has caused the attacker to land with his back to you, you should follow up immediately with an Upward Front kick to the groin from behind. As the opponent crouches in pain, you are in the ideal position for painful takedown: grab his ankles and pull them up while head-butting his lower back. As he fells on his face, you can stomp one of his ankles to make sure he will not have the ability to keep aggressing you.

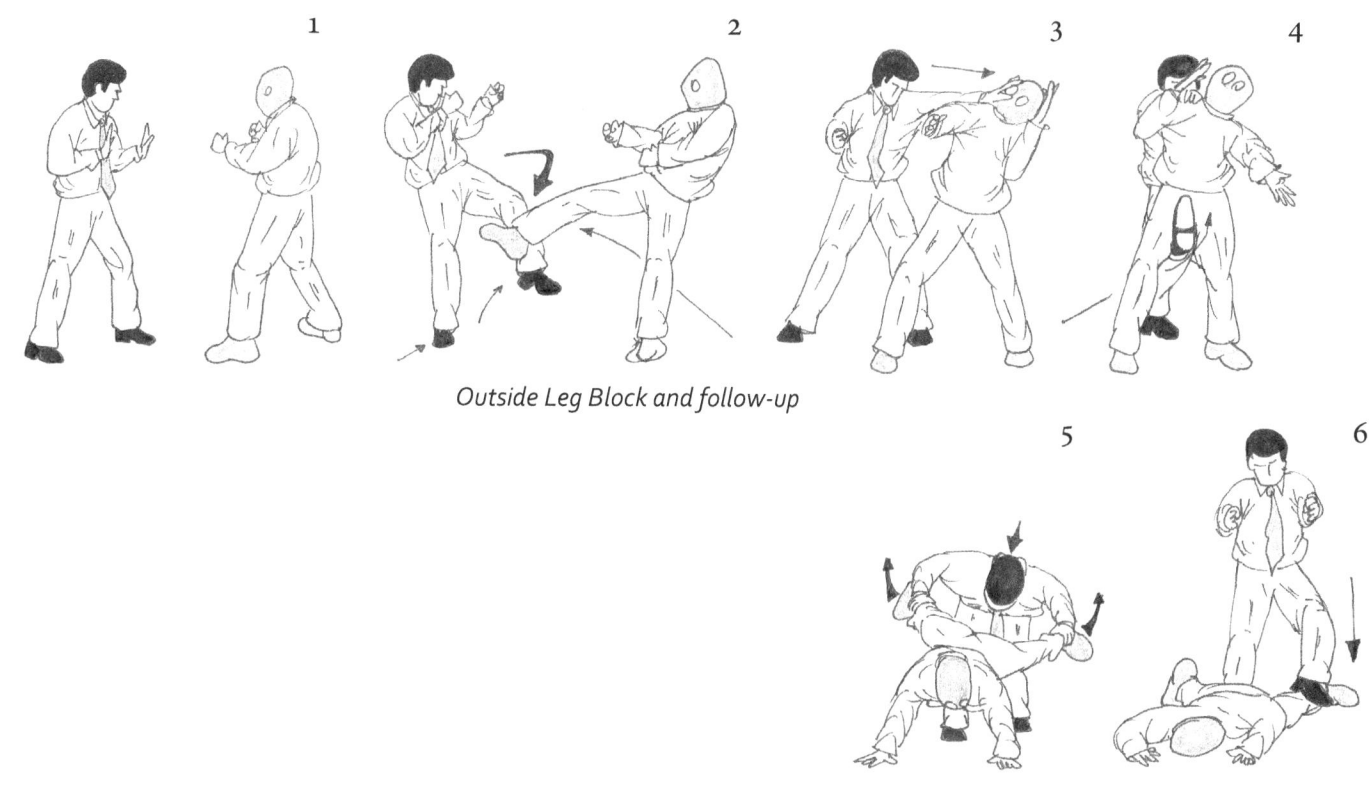

Outside Leg Block and follow-up

4.2 Defenses against Roundhouse Kicks

Defenses against Roundhouse Kicks are based on the same principles of the defenses against the Front Kick previously discussed. The principles stay the same, but with the necessary adaptations. We will cover a few examples briefly, and the reader will easily make the connection and devise his own preferred techniques.

The only additional principle to take into account is that the safest spot, when attacked with a Circular Kick, *is as close as possible to the axis around which the kick develops*. That means in practice, **close to the opponent**. Diving *to the inside* of an attacker in the midst of developing a Roundhouse is a very simple and effective tactic.

If you have come late to the party, and if the kick is already well on its way, the way to block a Roundhouse is illustrated below. This arms set-up is the best possible, because the height at which a Roundhouse connects is easily modified until the last seconds before impact. On top of that, this arms configuration allows for an easy scooping of the kicking leg for the fierce follow-ups that we shall present.

Multipurpose Blocking configuration to deal with Roundhouse Kicks

DEFENSES AGAINST KICKS

A. Preemptive

The coming Photos illustrate a *Preemptive Front Pushing Kick* to the thigh of the developing Roundhouse kick. Of course, following up is required.

Stop Kick to the incoming leg

A much more pitiless 'Krav Maga' approach, would be to stop-kick with a *Preemptive Upward Front Kick to the exposed groin* of the attacker. Your kick is fast and direct; his is circular and more cumbersome. See the Photos.

Kick the groin of the attacker before he can fully develop his Roundhouse; follow up

The downside of the previous elegant technique is that, should you miss the groin, you have not stopped anything and are vulnerable. The best alternative option if you are not yet sure of yourself enough, would be to kick his groin, but with a powerful Pushing or Penetrating Front Kick. The idea is to both to stop him by kicking near his center of gravity, and to shock him in the groin area with a reverberating hit. So, as illustrated in the Drawings at the top of next page, you execute a straight Front Kick towards his groin and connect with the heel or the sole of your shoe. Follow up with a Palm Strike to the face or chin, a grab of his head, a Knee Strike to the groin and an Uppercut Back Kick to his face as he crouches from pain (and is maintained there by your hand).

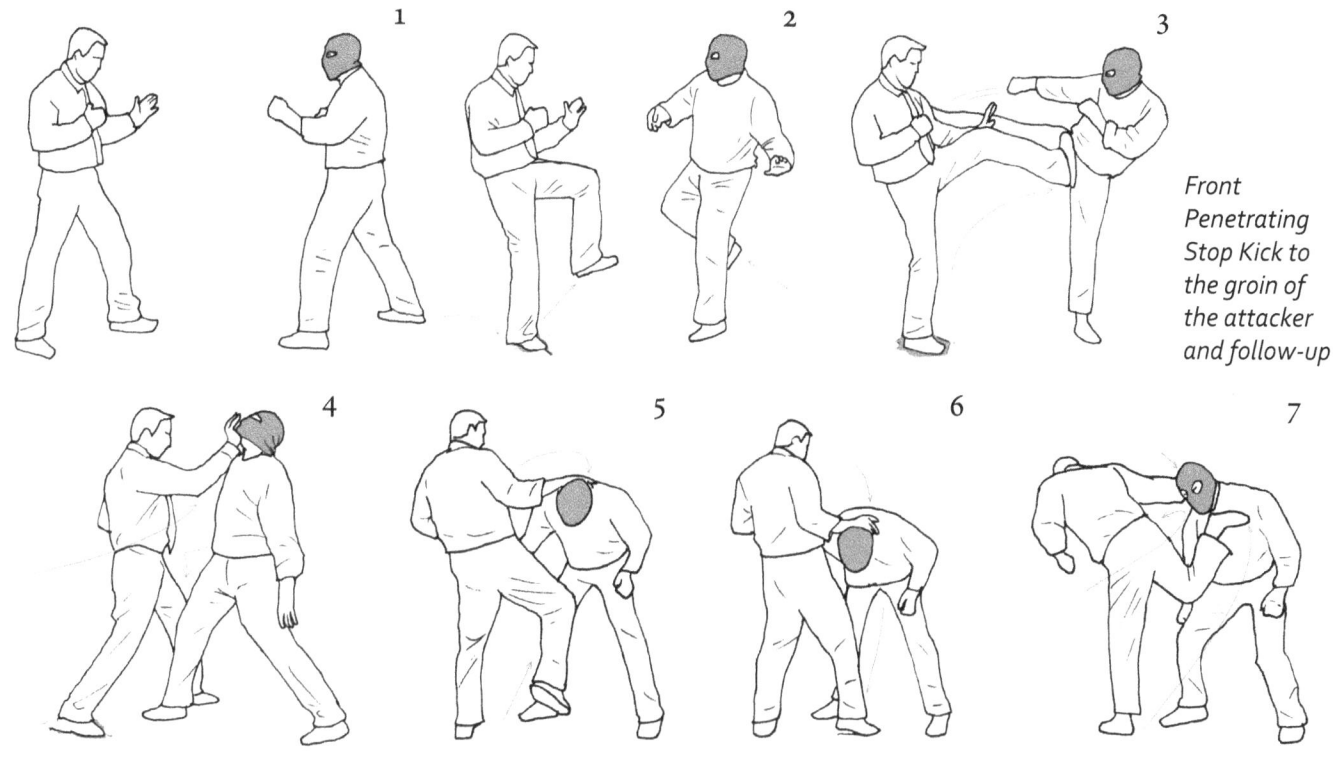

Front Penetrating Stop Kick to the groin of the attacker and follow-up

B. Evade/Block and Counter

The principles for *countering after evading and/or blocking* stay the same as for the Front Kick studied above. Just remember that the safe evasion against a Roundhouse is <u>diagonally forward to the inside of the kicking leg</u>, and that the closer you'll be to the attacker's kicking axis, the safer.

You could just hop there and punch, but it is safer to block, or at least take the covered position described at the beginning of the section. But from there, any counter goes, as the opponent is in a very vulnerable position.

We shall just present the use of the very punishing **Reaping Takedowns**, as counters. Just like with the front Kick, it is the best way to follow up, as the fall is very harsh for the opponent if you execute the Takedown aggressively: lift legs high and push upper body down. The coming sets of Illustrations, on the next page, are self-explanatory.

Evade and 'Block' the Roundhouse attack, knee the groin, reap his standing leg, throw his upper body towards the floor and punch his exposed groin

Slightly different variation: Evade and 'Block', deliver a Front-leg Upward Side Kick to the groin, reap while twisting (Harai Goshi style), and stomp the exposed groin

KRAV MAGA KICKS

C. Leg Block

The Leg Block is also effective against Roundhouses targeting the mid-body or lower. It is also a good tactic if you are late at dealing with the incoming kick. The Photos below illustrate such a *Leg Block*, followed by a Spin-back short Back Kick to the groin and an Elbow Strike to the face (face on its way down from the pain of the testicles). Keep the *Retzev* going as long as necessary. Spin-backs are not very common in *Krav Maga*, because there is usually a safer alternative; but in this case. The Leg Block has an inherent twisting momentum that is best used for a fast spin.

Leg Block against a mid-level Roundhouse, with a Spin-back counter

4.3 Defenses against Side Kicks

The reader is now familiar with the general principles of defending against kicking attacks. **Dealing with Side Kicks** is based on the same principles and the trainee will fast realize that. Side Kicks are usually executed from the front leg, with a step or a hop. But Side Kicks are a little particular in that they are usually easier to spot early because the preparatory stance is sideways and the chambering is quite specific. Dealing with the Side Kick can also easily lead to 'owning' the opponent's back. But, it should also be remembered that a successful Side Kick is one of the most powerful strikes possible, in terms of energy delivered. Caution then!
We shall now present a few defenses, with no special emphasis on the classification.

The most effective way to deal with the Side Kick will be, of course, **<u>preemptively</u>** with a *Stop Kick*.

The first set of Illustrations show a '**Stop-the-kick**' approach, in which you use your own Side Kick to strike its chambering leg. A front-leg Side Kick will generally be executed from a Side Stance, after a high hand feint that covers a forward hop. You will foil the attacker's plans by reacting to the high feint to boost his confidence, but then hopping yourself fast forward to for a *Low Side Stop Kick into his legs*. The opponent does not expect you to go forward and will be still in his development for a 'long' kick. Aim for the knee, like in the Photo and the Drawings, and then follow-up immediately: a rear-leg powerful Low Kick to the knee, a hip-driven Circular Elbow Strike to the face, and an Outer Reap Takedown. And keep at it, if necessary, by stomping his ankles and/or elbows.

Stop the Kick by blocking his chambering leg

Stop a Stop Kick with a forward-hopping Low Side Stop Kick to the opponent's kicking leg on its way to chamber; then follow up

If you are slightly late, or if you feel more comfortable, you can also stop-kick him *at the hip* to interrupt his momentum and to prevent him to be able to extend the kick. See Drawings below. You can in fact aim grossly towards the place of the chambered knee: if you get the knee, fine; if you miss the knee you stop him at the hip, fine too. In both cases, the attackers will be put off-balance rearwards. You can follow up with a long rear-leg powerful kick-through Roundhouse Kick towards his kidneys (lower back). From then on, start your *Retzev*.

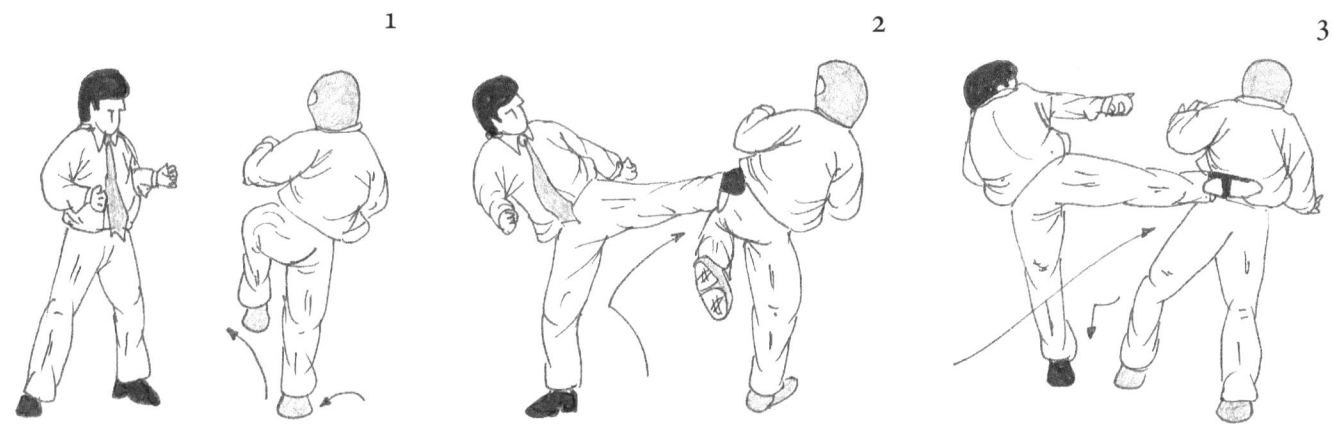

Stop-kick the hip of an assailant hopping forward for a Side Kick attack

The second-best way to deal with the Side kick is the **Forward Evasion**, usually with some form of blocking/controlling/covering. As mentioned, it is more advantageous to go for the *outside* of the kicking leg, which will drive him to present his back, and therefore his blind side. It is not always possible but should be strived for.

The Illustrations, at the top of next page, show how to step deep *forward and out*, while covering yourself in an arm set-up identical to the general Roundhouse Defense. This is for added security. The follow-up presented is a simple Head-pushing Takedown: grab him, even before his kicking foot lands, and strike his nose with you Palm. Keep your hand on his face, fingers in the general eyes area, and tilt his head back to push it directly down towards the floor. In a serious confrontation the push is brusque and violent; and you also go all the way to slam his head into the floor. **<u>Extreme caution is warranted in training: go slowly and with control</u>**.

Evade forward and out, and catch his head for a hard Takedown

DEFENSES AGAINST KICKS

The same evading move lends itself to other hard Takedowns, as will be illustrated in the two next sets of Figures. The **covered forward-and-out Evasion** is ideal for scooping the kicking leg, just as we saw with the Roundhouse Kick Defenses.

In the first example, you scoop and lift the leg up while delivering a *Knee Strike to the open groin*. Lower the foot for a hip-powered Sweep of the attacker's standing leg. Lift his leg and body <u>while sweeping him at hip height with your thigh</u>; the rest of the leg sweeping his thigh. Lift him *as high as possible* and push his body forcefully down during the fall to cause a hard impact. Follow-up by stomping if needed.

Scoop his Leg for a Sweeping Takedown

In the same set-up, you could also throw him down with an even harder *Reaping Takedown*. The Drawings at the top of next page illustrate how the Evasion becomes a *Leg Scoop* and then, after the *Groin Knee*, you reap his standing leg to make him fall forward 'on his face'. As he lands in this precarious position, you can still Downward-elbow his groin before pushing his legs forcefully down and away. <u>**Be very careful in training, this is a very nasty fall.**</u>

➡

Scoop his leg for a Reaping hard Takedown

Of course, just to be complete, it should be clear that evading to the *inside*, or evading *without coverage* are also valid *Krav Maga* approaches; they simply require more proficiency and training. In the Photos below, the Side Kick attack is evaded normally to the *Outside*. But, instead of a Block or a Covering move, you strike the attacking knee with a Downward Forearm. This is a painful attack of the knee in kicking extension. Follow-up with a Palm Strike to the side of the head (Ear/Temple/Jaw Hinge), and get him into a Rear Naked Choke.

Evade and strike the kicking leg

DEFENSES AGAINST KICKS

If you have been taken by surprise and can neither stop-kick nor evade forward, you'll have no choice but **evading rearwards**.

In the first set of Drawings, you see how to step back while pulling your belly back out of range. You 'block' the incoming kick by deviating its trajectory to the opponent's inside. Let your retreating leg rebound on the floor to come back forward immediately, for a Stomping Side Kick into the side/back of the standing knee of the attacker. Kick the knee *into* the ground and grind it there. You should try to scoop the kicking leg at the end of the block, if possible, and keep hold of it. That will place you in much better control when the opponent will reach the floor: you can twist his ankle and/or kick his open groin.

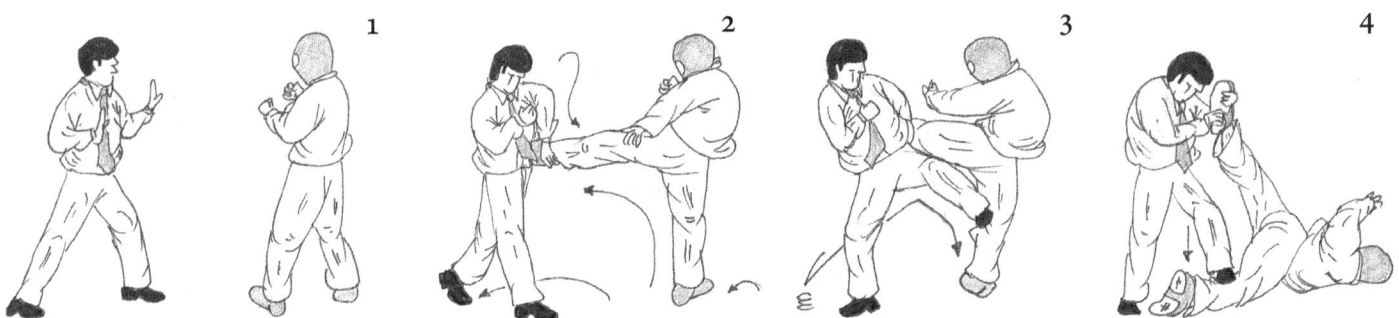

Step back to evade rearwards and scoop the kicking foot before coming back forward with a Knee Stomping Kick

If you are taken even more unawares, then your instinctive reaction would be **to jump back while pulling the midsection in** and while *striking down the incoming foot*. Use this natural reaction to do just that, but striking the incoming leg down and *towards the attacker's inside*. Counter immediately with an Upward Front Kick to the opponent's groin, from behind. Follow up!

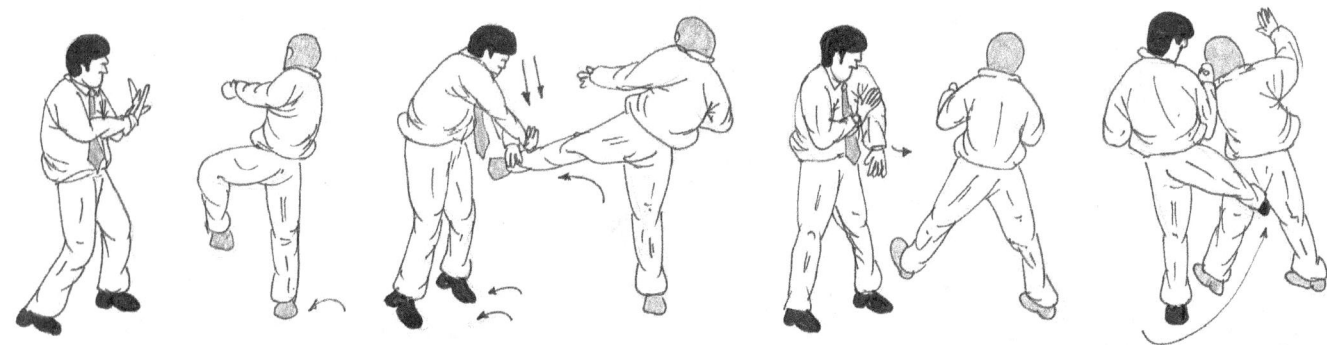

Pull back and strike the kicking foot down and sideways; follow up

4.4 Defenses against Low Kicks

The 'Low Kick' is used a lot in *Krav Maga*, for the simple reason that it is very effective, especially when targeting the knee with precision. It is therefore very important to deal with Low Kick attacks, and there are basically 3 ways to do that: **preempt**, **evade** or **block**.

1. <u>Preemption</u> can be an early attack before the Low Kick is in serious development, or it can be an early Stop Kick to the attacking leg. It should be noted that preemption of a Low Kick is pretty difficult because of its inherent speed and short warning window. As illustrated in the first series of drawings, it is easier when your adversary is a 'serial' user of the technique. In this example, you evade rearwards a first Low Kick, and then get ready to *preempt* the next one. As soon as you 'feel' the very beginning of the attack, go forward with your own Shin Front Pushing Kick to the floating ribs. Keep protected and kick, do not push. You can follow up with hip-powered Circular Elbow Strikes to the sides of the head. And finish with a Ghost Kick to the testicles.

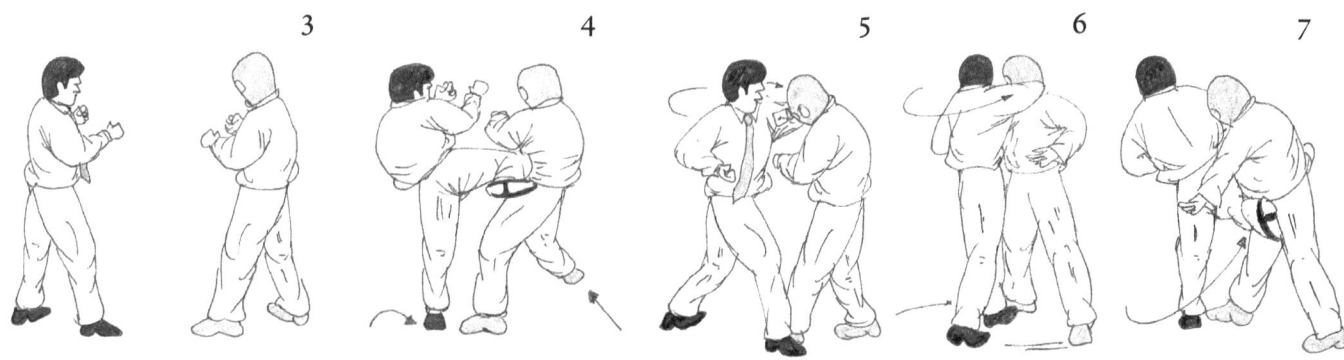

Preempt with an early forward-going Stop Kick

If you are fast and confident, you can also simply *kick towards the opponent's groin* with all you have as early as possible.

Preemptive Groin Stop Kick as soon as you 'feel' the opponent's decision to attack

DEFENSES AGAINST KICKS

Of course, you can also *stop-punch* early; it is usually faster, but safety commands some evading. You should go *forward diagonally* to take some distance from the incoming Low Kick. It is pretty easy but requires familiarization and training. In the first set of drawings below, you go diagonally forward against a Low Kick to your inner front knee. Simultaneously poke towards the attacker's eyes and lift your rear foot directly into his groin while his kicking leg is still airborne. Keep at it if necessary.

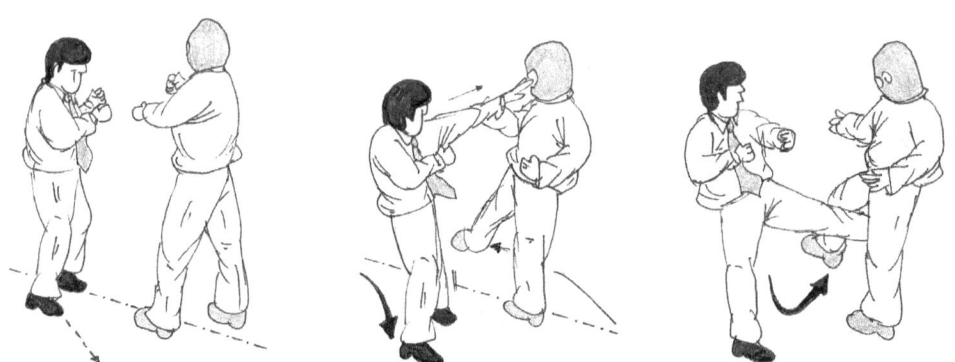

Attack the opponent's eyes while going diagonally forward and follow up

Another example is illustrated in the Figures below. The evasion is identical, but you will punch the chin of the rushing attacker. The following Groin Kick is also more powerful: it is hip powered and aims at kicking <u>through the groin into the upper thigh of the standing leg.</u>

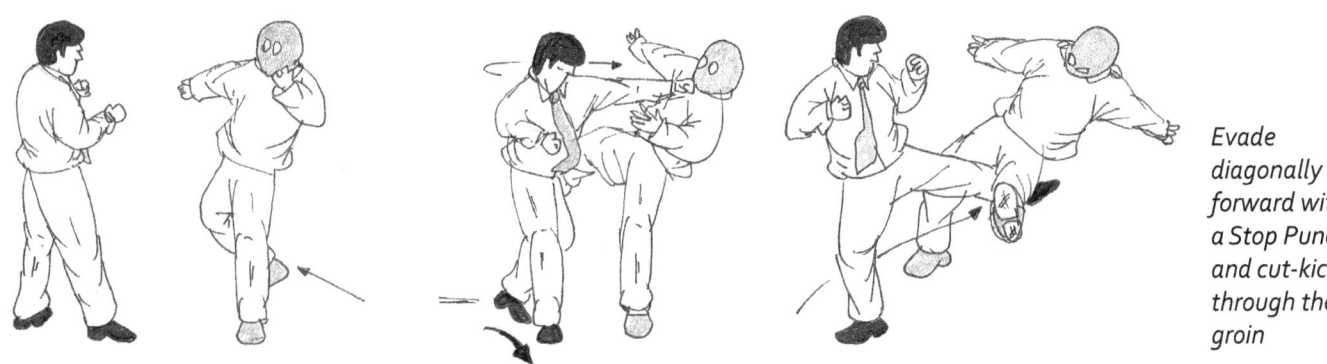

Evade diagonally forward with a Stop Punch and cut-kick through the groin

2. <u>Evasion</u> *is elegant and natural*: you just pull back the targeted leg. The principle is simple, but it is not always easy to pull the leg fast enough. Training and free-fighting are required. Once you have removed the leg from the kicking trajectory, you should try to make good use of the opponent's momentum and probable (slight) loss of balance.

In the example illustrated below, you pull the targeted leg back to let the Low Kick pass and you let your foot rebound on the floor for a counterattack. You counter by kicking the back knee of the attacking leg, and by doing so you amplify the opponent's momentum. Make sure you target the knee, and not the thigh, for maximum damage. Your well-timed Low Kick will allow you to land deep behind the attacker. Grab his shoulders for a simple Groin Kick from behind and take him down with a naturally-following Kicking Sweep of his rear ankle (pull his opposite shoulder simultaneously). Stomp his ankles, hands or head if necessary.

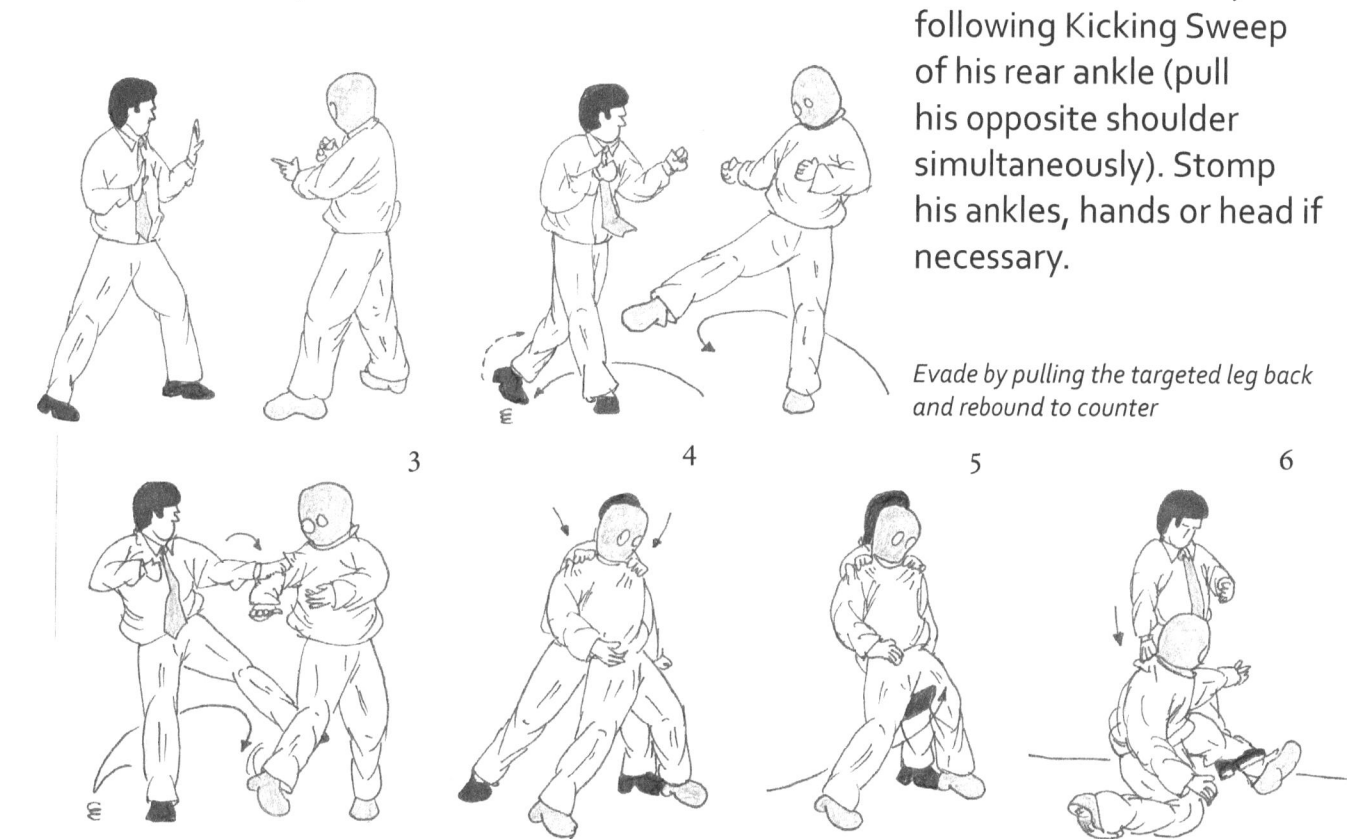

Evade by pulling the targeted leg back and rebound to counter

The reader should note that many other counters are possible once the leg has been pulled out of the Low Kick's trajectory; he is invited to try his own 'Retzev'.

3. **<u>Blocking</u>** *is simple, fast and effective.* But it requires some training to make it automatic and to learn to deal with the fact that it can be somewhat painful. You simply lift the leg to block the incoming Low Kick with the fleshier part of the lower leg. A slightly circular movement at the end of the Leg Block helps absorbing the direct hit. It should be noted that this classical *Leg Block* can be executed with the front or the rear leg, and that it is also valid against a mid-body Roundhouse Kick.

The classic Leg Block

DEFENSES AGAINST KICKS

The front-leg Leg Block

The rear-leg Leg Block

Of course, what is important is what will follow the *Leg Block*. The Illustrations below show how you leg-block the 'Low Kick' and immediately counterpunch while landing the blocking foot forward. Your forward momentum is key to the success of this defense. Your mind and body must be in offensive '**assault**' mode (in Hebrew: הסתערות). Follow up with no hesitation: a rear-leg Roundhouse Kick to the groin, completed with a Low Kick of your own to the opponent's knee joint. Continue if necessary.

Leg Block with quasi-simultaneous Punch to the throat or chin; and follow-up

144   **KRAV MAGA KICKS**

If you are fast and can stop the Low Kick early, it is even better to **Stop Kick the incoming leg** in the initial stages of the attack. This classic Leg Block (of the type: **Stopping-the-leg Stop Kick**) requires more training and experience, but is even more effective than the more 'passive' Leg Block described above.

The Illustrations show how to use a *front-leg Front Pushing Stop Kick* to intercept the knee of the developing Low Kick. Kick hard and follow up immediately: A Punch or a Palm Strike to the nose as you land forward, and then a Groin Kick and a Knee Strike to the face of the opponent bending in pain.

Another Leg Block: Stop Front Kick to the knee of the developing Low Kick

4.5 Defenses against Knee Strikes

Krav Maga makes ample use of the **Knee Strike to the groin** because it is both simple and extremely effective. It is important to learn to 'see' the preliminaries to a Knee Strike in order to avoid it at all costs: once kneed in the testicles, your fighting chance is as good as gone.

Therefore, you should *always strike preemptively anyone trying to get into your close fighting range*. In close combat range, it is usually the first to strike who scores, no matter how good you are. Keep fanatically your safety distance and whip-strike the eyes or kick the shins of anyone trying to weasel himself too close.

...If your opponent nevertheless is close enough to launch a Knee Strike, your own knee **should already be on the way**! Or an eye poke. Or a Palm Strike.

If you find yourself anyway in a clinch for some reason, it is wise to control the hip of the opponent with your forearm and to press down when the Knee comes up, as it certainly must. Take your hips back and sideways for extra caution, and follow up. You could follow up with a Palm Strike to the groin, or to the throat. Anything goes, and should be followed by a merciless *Retzev*.

Evade back and out, and press the opponent's hip down to control the Knee Strike

A follow-up that makes use of the Knee Strike itself is presented below. As your opponent graciously 'gives' you his raised knee, you can scoop it up with your other hand for a very harsh Takedown. Lift his scooped knee and sweep his standing ankle while lifting his body as high as possible. Then throw his head and upper body violently towards the floor while keeping his leg high.

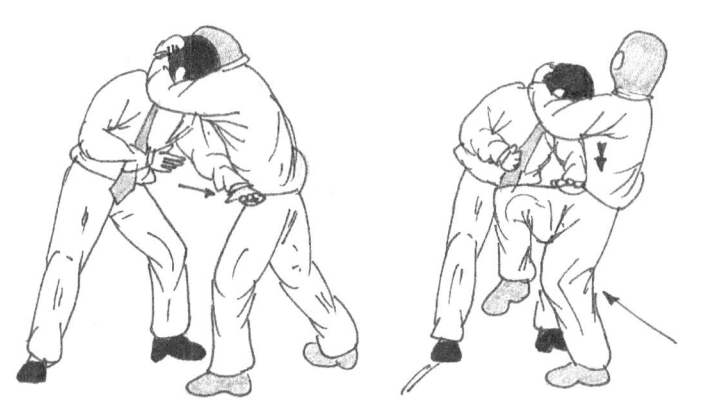

Control and scoop his knee for a violent takedown

3   4   5   6

146   **KRAV MAGA KICKS**

As you will make sure to keep potential assailants away (!), most Knee attacks will come from middle range and will require some preparations and footwork from the opponent. This will allow you to handle them in the same way you would handle a kick. In fact, a Knee Strike is not different from the chambering of a Front Kick. You should therefore evade out while controlling (and deviating) the Knee Strike, either with the leg or with the hand.

The first Figures illustrate how to **leg-block**, coming from the outside in, the incoming Knee Strike. Nearly simultaneously, extend your front hand into his eyes. Catch his head by the hair, the ear, the nose, or anything possible, and pull his head back to 'open' his *throat* to an incoming 'chop' (*Knife-hand Strike*). As he is flustered and as you 'own' his back, you can set a Rear Naked Choke. Make sure you use your elbow as a vise from which you press his carotid arteries from both sides. Be careful to release the hold as soon as the opponent loses consciousness: **_this is a very dangerous and potentially lethal hold, to be used only in extreme cases of self-defense. CAUTION._**

Leg-block a Knee Strike and lash out for the eyes first

The next set of Drawings, at the top of next page, illustrates how to pivot and slightly **evade out**, while controlling/blocking the attack with the hand. Go forward into his momentum with a Forearm or Ridge-hand Strike to the neck, very much like a 'Clothesline' manoeuver. Keep control of his neck (in a choke-like hold) and use his lack of balance to reap his standing leg in a classic Takedown (O Soto Guruma). Twist him over your hip and lift his leg as high as possible to make him fall on his head. Keep at it with stomps if necessary.

➡

Evade and block, for an immediate forward-charging Clothesline Strike

And a last word about Groin Knee Strikes. The groin being such a sensitive target (as mentioned in a previous Part), it is important to be always conscious of its vulnerability and of its situation vis-à-vis the opponent. By keeping your upper thighs squeezed together, you can prevent the success of most groin attack. Try it and learn to use this simple trick in any case in which you are in potential danger of a groin attack. There are several major *Karate* styles built around a posture called '*Sanchin Dachi*' (The Hourglass Posture) that keeps the thighs squeezed together and makes their disciples very impervious to groin kicks and knee strikes. The constant use of this posture requires serious training, but the *Krav Maga Artist* will simply remember the trick.

Sanchin Dachi
- The Hourglass Posture of Okinawan Karate

Nobody's a natural. You work hard to get good and then work to get better. It's hard to stay on top.
~Paul Coffey

5. Defenses against Grabs

Grabs are not innocuous, they are aggressive invasions of your personal space and they are generally the beginning of a more serious attack. You have to react immediately to neutralize the danger and to free yourself from an unlawful restraint on your freedom of movement.

5.1 Wrist Grabs

a. Grabs with one hand

We shall present the classic release maneuvers against **Wrist Grabs**. The basic principle is very simple: twist the wrist to place the narrowest side in front of the gap between the opponent's thumb and his other fingers, and pull. There is a little more than that, but we'll come back to it after an important introduction.

If someone grabs your wrist in a clear self-defense situation, **do not try to free the grabbed wrist!** First of all: strike your assailant. That's right, forget about pulling your wrist out. At least until later!

When someone grabs your wrist, you are being attacked (unless it is drunken uncle Charlie). The wrist grab is not only an invasion of your personal space, an unagreed restriction of your freedom of movement, a bullying action and so on; it is above all the beginning of an attack. It causes you to focus your attention on your wrist and it restricts your ability to defend yourself. Something is going on, and it is very possible that a punch or a kick is already on its way to you. If you concentrate to free your arm, you'll be hit; if you try to use your other hand to deflect an attack, you are limited and put off-balance by the grab.

Therefore, if you have allowed someone to get close enough by refraining from preemptive strikes, and if he then grabs your wrist(s), there is only one thing to do: **Strike immediately in the most punishing way possible**. Only lashing out at once and aggressively will allow the foiling of the aggressor's plans and the dimming of the attack probably on its way to you.

Remember also that the 'grabber' is not necessarily alone. Strike, free yourself and look around.

We shall now explain the basic principles of freeing your wrist from a grab. Keep in mind that these small arm moves will come **after** you have struck your assailant and during the *Retzev* that must follow. It should be an instinctive releasing move made easy by the fact that your opponent has been mollified by previous strikes.

The *principles* are simple, and stay valid for all situations:
- Twist the grabbed wrist in order to place the narrow side towards the 'gap' between the opponent's thumb and his other fingers.
- Pull the wrist through the gap.
- Pull by rotating your hand on an axis that is close to the grabbing hand: by doing so you use an effective fulcrum to release yourself.
- Pull then with your body and not with your arm only.
- Do this after neutralizing the threat.

The first set of Figures below illustrates the basic release technique in a classic **opposite-hand**-grabbing situation.

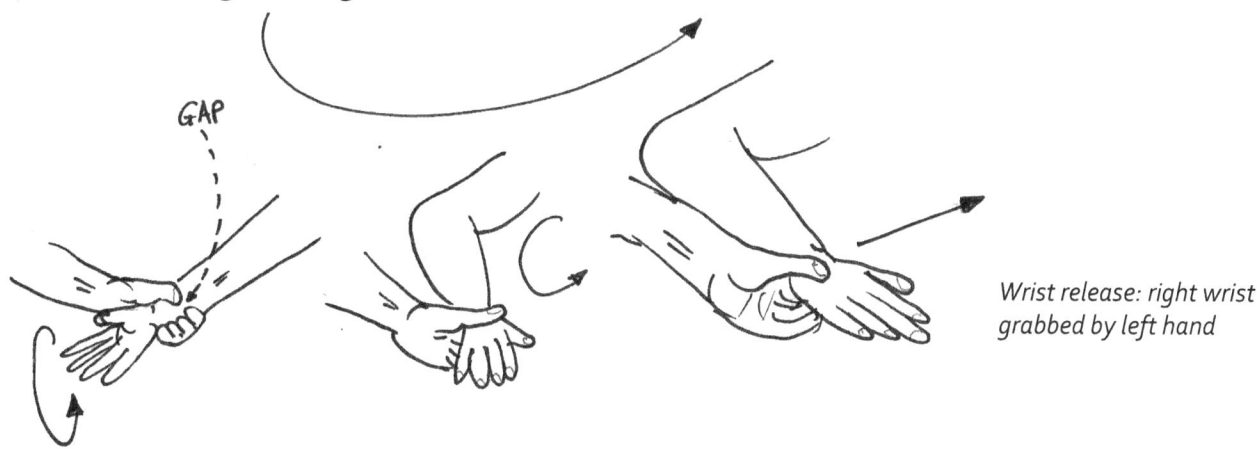

Wrist release: right wrist grabbed by left hand

The second set of Drawings shows the release based on the same principles, but for a **same-hand**-grabbing situation.

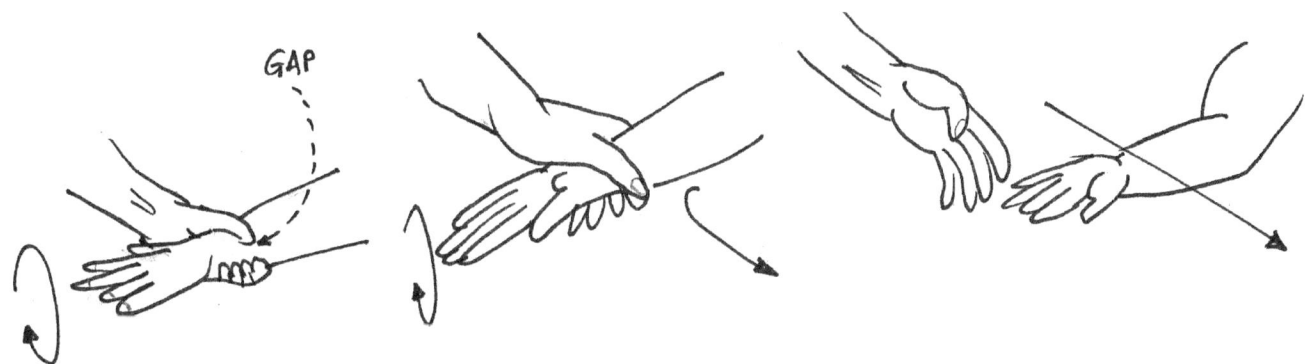

DEFENSES AGAINST GRABS

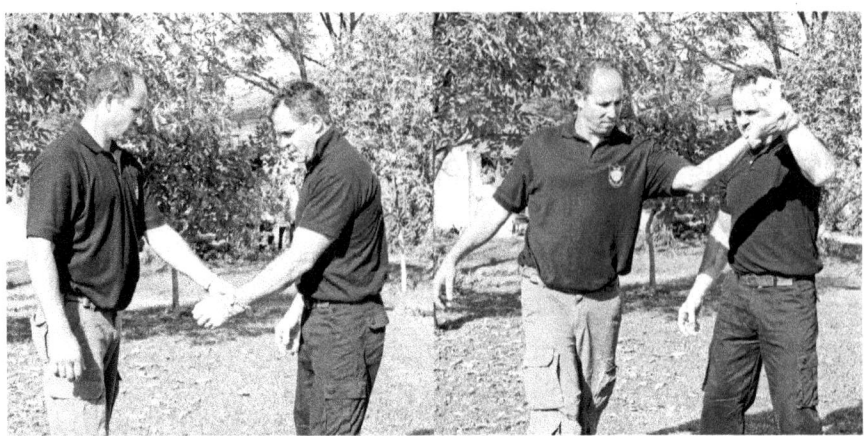

Left wrist release. After a preventive strike!

Right wrist release with follow-up. Remember that the release comes after a protective strike

Now, the next phase is to understand that these releases can also be helped by a simultaneous strike on to the grabbing wrist. All principles stay valid: first strike to stop any attack, then release through the gap. See next page…

Opposite grab: Slap the wrist as you pull through the gap and follow up

Hard Knife-hand Strike on to the forearm as you pull the wrist through the 'gap'. Strike to hurt, and then follow up

Violent Knife-hand Strike to the grabbing forearm while you pull the wrist through the 'gap' for release. Start your Retzev with a Knife-hand Strike to the side of the neck and a Palm Strike to the face.

DEFENSES AGAINST GRABS

And now we put it all together...

In the first example, illustrated below, an assailant grabs your wrist with his opposite hand. Is he just fooling around? Is he going to pull you towards him? Is he going to punch you? ... Who cares? You immediately *front-kick his groin* and execute the Wrist Release technique while lowering back your kicking leg. Let your kicking foot rebound on the floor to help launch a Knee Strike to the face of the crouching opponent. Pull his head down with your hands for a more effective strike. And keep his head down for a Hammer-fist or Forearm Strike to the neck.

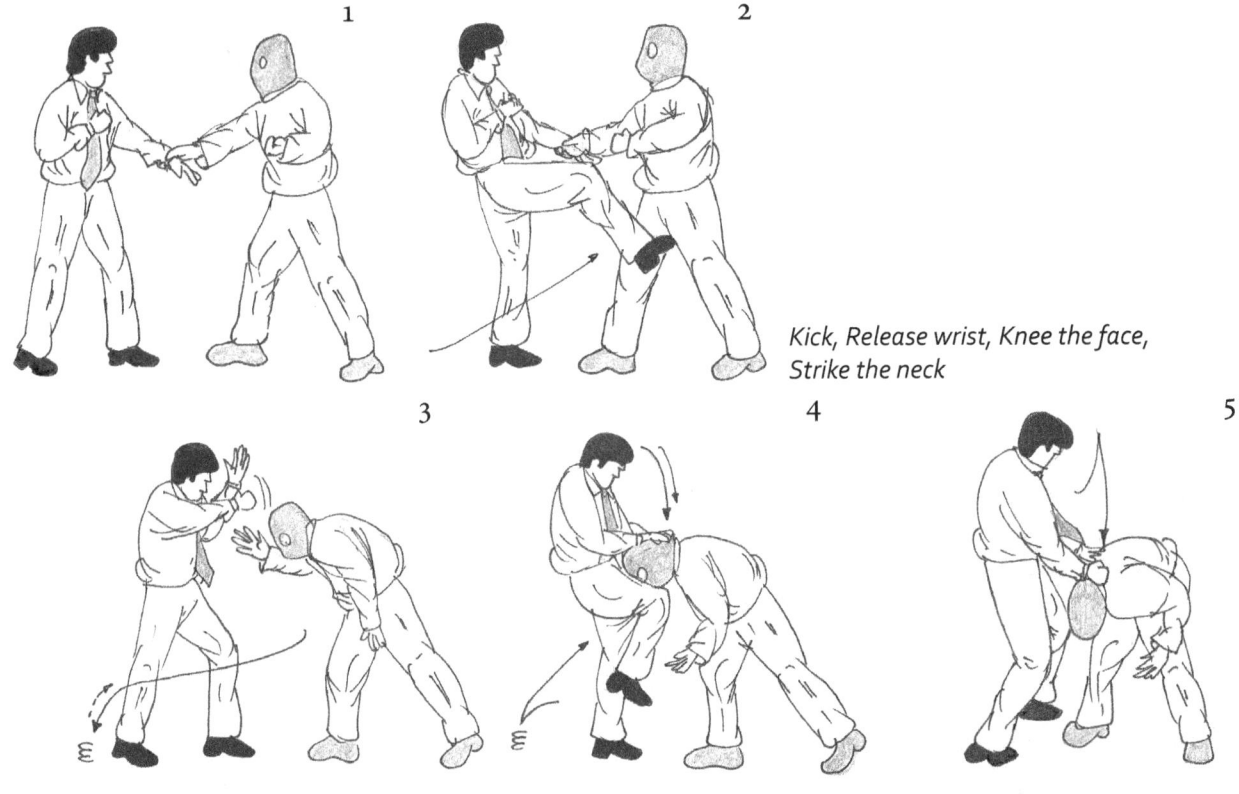

Kick, Release wrist, Knee the face, Strike the neck

If the assailant grabs your right wrist with his right hand (*same-side grab*), you should immediately whip his eyes to prevent any strike and to mollify him before your release. The release technique follows the principles presented at the start of the Chapter for same-side grab, *but you simultaneously step out and you slap his grabbing elbow from the outside.* Your freed hand comes back immediately for a violent Palm Strike a few inches into his groin area. As he bends down in pain, push him down forward while kicking his front ankle back and up. Immediately follow up by stomping his Achille's ligament. This is all illustrated at the top of next page.

➤

Attack the eyes, Release while also slapping the elbow; Palm-strike the groin; Sweep-kick the ankle; Stomp the exposed Achille's Tendon

The next set of Drawings illustrates, again, a defense against a wrist grab *with the same hand*. You immediately fast-whip the opponent's eyes, and then use the same hand to strike down the opponent's forearm in a 'Downward Block' fashion (*Gedan Barai – Karatedo*). This is not a Block, but a **Strike** meaning to hurt, and you simultaneously pull your grabbed hand out according to the principles of wrist release presented above. You follow up immediately with a very natural hip-powered Palm Strike to the chin or the nose. You could continue with an Outward Ghost Groin Kick that allows you to move on or check your surroundings.

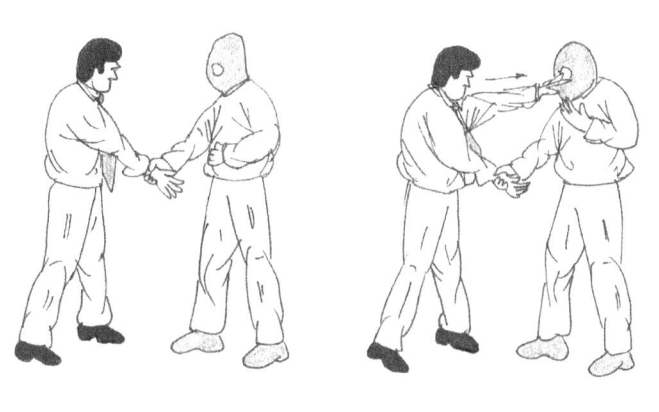

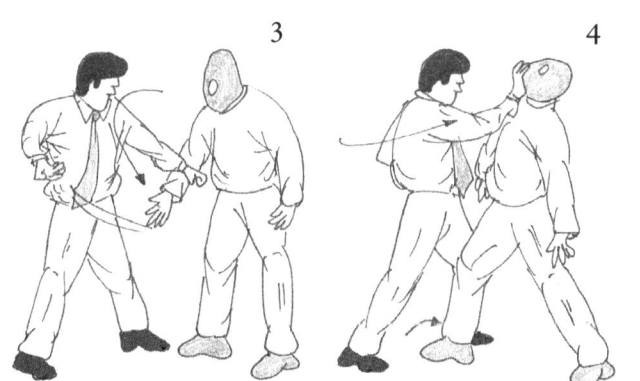

Whip the eyes, Strike the forearm while releasing, Palm-strike the face, Kick the groin

DEFENSES AGAINST GRABS

The coming Illustrations show another kind of technique against a *same-side grab*. You immediately step slightly forward with an Eye Poke or an Eye Whip. You use the forward movement to start encircling his wrist from the outside, but you step back at once while completing the '*counter-grab*'. Kick him in the groin and palm-strike his face as you lower the foot. You are now in perfect position to push him down in a classic Armlock. The Armlock can be used to control him, or it can be a Strike to the extended elbow to damage the joint

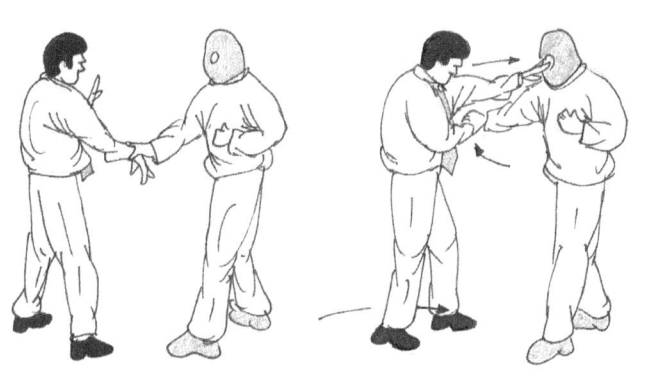

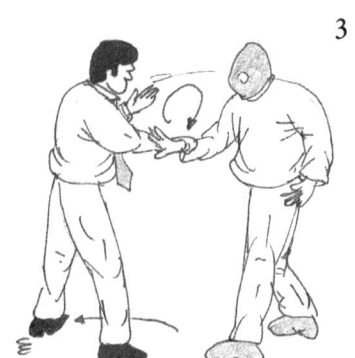
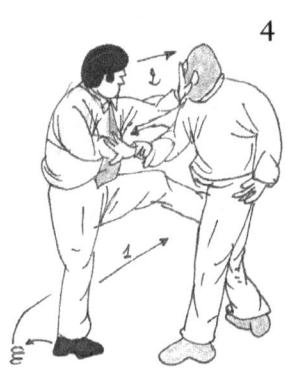

Poke the eyes, Reverse the grab, Kick the groin, Palm-strike the face, Set an arm-lock

This 'Counter-grab' technique (based on the 'Ni-kyo' Second Principle of *Aikido*) is simple and answers to all Principles of Release already mentioned. The release technique can end in the Counter-grab, or simply in the Knife-hand 'cutting' through his wrist, as illustrated below. In the same-side grab situation, you circle his grabbing hand from the outside while twisting your wrist. It is best done while pulling the arm towards yourself. You then invert the twisting of the hand to place the Knifehand side towards the grabbing wrist. You then start pushing back towards the opponent, while 'cutting' through his wrist (or while counter-grabbing his wrist). If you cut violently you can also cause him some joint damage while releasing your wrist.

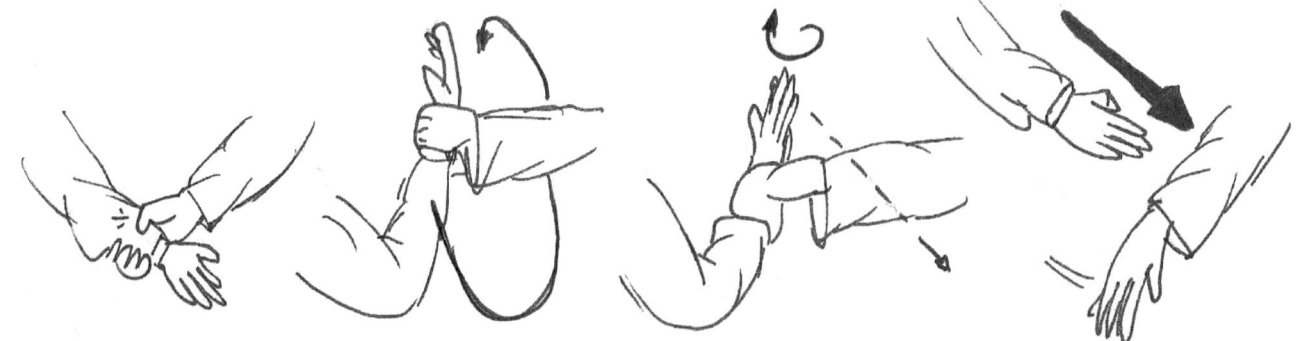

*The 'No counter-grab' version of the release technique: cut violently **through** the grabbing wrist!*

And we shall finish this section with an example in the spirit of the KISS principle. Simple is always best. An assailant grabs your wrist with the same hand. Pivot slightly to lift the front leg in Side Kick Chamber. You naturally pull back on your wrist. As he reacts to pull back on your pulling, he helps your momentum to crush his knee. You simultaneously release your wrist according to the basic principles described. Follow up, preferably by stomping his joints.

He grabs and you simply side-kick his knee

b. Grabs with two hands

When your opponent uses **both hands** to grab one or both your wrists, he is not in a situation in which he can punch you fast. You should still beware of a kick, a knee strike or a head butt though. This is still a serious attack and an infringement on your freedom of movement. Maybe your are grabbed to give time for an accomplice to approach, or in order to pull you, or because you are holding a weapon or something that can be used as one. Wrist-grabbing can also be a way to close the gap safely: he will then release you suddenly and strike in close quarters.
You therefore have, again, to strike immediately to prevent any follow-up and to mollify him before your own escape technique.

b1. The release technique from *a grab of both your wrists* is identical to the 'opposite-side' grab release presented in the previous section: it is simply doubled and one side is the mirror image of the other. The release principles are identical. See Figures and Photos at the top of next page.

DEFENSES AGAINST GRABS

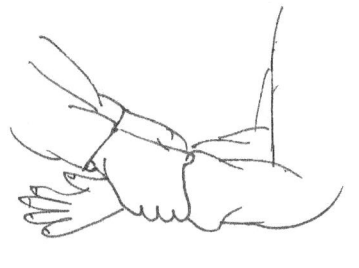  

Classic release technique of the two-wrists grab; of course, comes after a preventive strike

Double wrist grab release and follow-up of Groin Kick and Neck Hammer-fist Strike

An alternative to the classic double wrist grab release, *would be releasing only one wrist*. And your counter will certainly make him release the other one. In this version, you effect the classic **one-wrist** opposite-side release, while helping by striking the grabbing forearm with your other still-grabbed hand. It is quite simple, and the Photos below will make this much clearer.

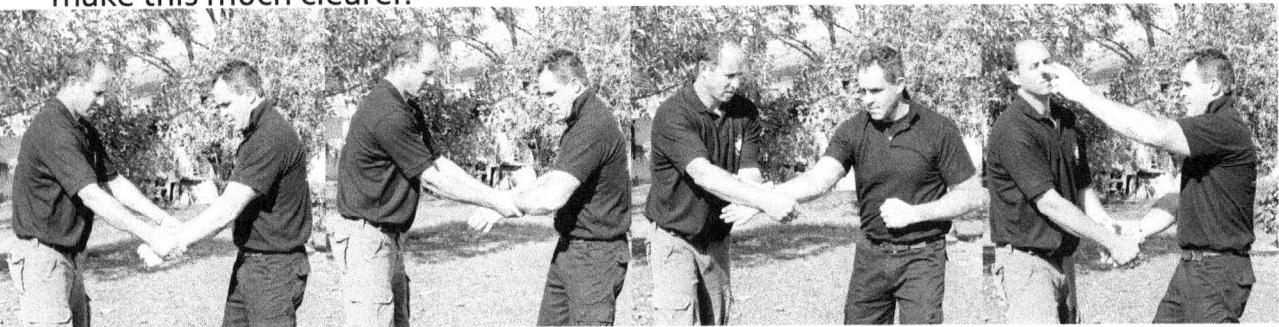

Use a grabbed hand to help the release of the other one; then, strike!

Okay! Let us now put everything together: preventive strikes, wrists release and follow-up. The Drawings below illustrate how to immediately head-butt the assailant's nose as he grabs your wrists. Do this *while pulling your wrists back towards you* to keep him close and to elicit a reaction. The instinctive reaction as you pull back, is to oppose the pull and to pull your wrists back to him. You use the momentum of his reaction to drive forward and strike his general groin area (or lower belly) with both fists. [Here is the place to mention that when you hurt a grabbing assailant, his instinctive reaction is NOT to release you even though he is hit; the atavistic instinctive reaction is to keep the grab, like a dog with his fangs into flesh]. Once you have punched his groin area, step deeply back while executing the classic wrists release. Follow up with a powerful rear-leg Groin Kick and start your *Retzev*.

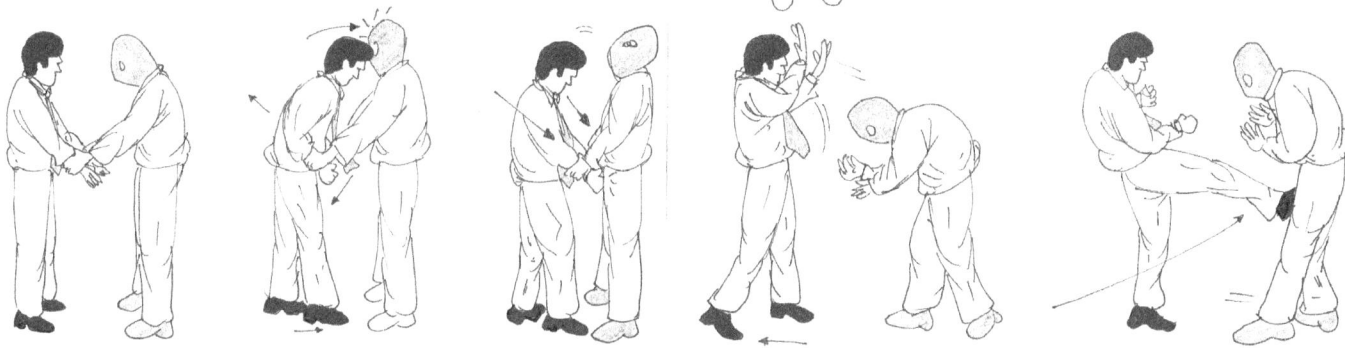

Head-butt, Punch groin, Release, Groin-kick

<u>**b2**</u>. The release technique from a ***single wrist grab with both hands*** is more specific. A classic release is not possible because the double grab is powerful and has no 'gap' to escape through. That also makes the preventive/mollifying attack even more important: Strike before the release in all cases!

The big advantage of this grab, from your point of view, is that both of the opponent's hands are busy. But remember: that it can be changing suddenly, that you could still be headbutted or kicked, that you could be violently pulled or placed off-balance... It is therefore a requisite, again, that you react immediately. After a preventive strike, you will make a fist with your grabbed hand, and come get grab the fist firmly with your other hand. You then use both arms (and your whole body) to pull the grabbed wrist up and away. The coming Photos illustrate the release technique and possible follow-up.

The release technique from a two-handed grab of your wrist, and Low Side Kick follow-up

DEFENSES AGAINST GRABS

The applied example illustrated by the Drawings below handles a slightly different grab: *one wrist and the second hand grabs the arm of the same side*. This has no bearing on the release technique, but it is there to show that small variations of the attacks should not require other techniques if the principles are respected. The defense presented in the example is simple: kick the opponent's *groin* immediately as he grabs you. Do not wait to be pulled or placed into an Arm-lock! The example shows a Penetrating Tilted-foot Front Kick to the general groin area, but it could be any other Front Kick towards the testicles. You can then execute the classic release presented above. Follow-up immediately with a Circular hip-powered Elbow strike to the side of his head. Grab his head, preferably by slapping both his ears, while throwing a very naturally-flowing Knee Groin Strike.

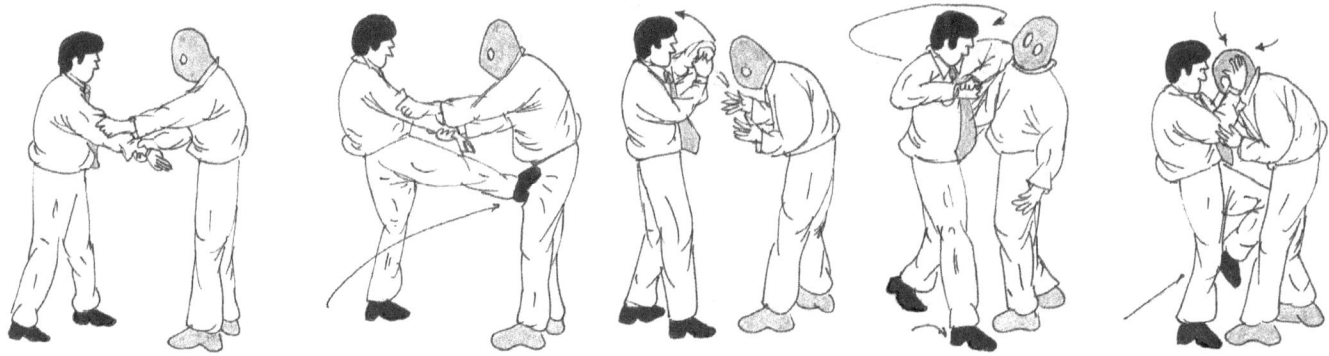

Groin Kick, Release, Elbow Strike, Groin Kick with Twin Ear Palm Strike

5.2 Lapel Grab

When someone **grabs your lapel**, it means that he is much too close and has dodgy intentions. The situation is like for the wrist grabs: although it does not hurt you yet, it is a potentially very dangerous situation: you could be struck, pulled around, pushed to the wall, or simply immobilized until accomplices arrive.

In this day and age of gratuitous violence, you cannot take the risk to hesitate: the first punch could already be on his way. A preventive strike is needed in all cases, and at once. Just like for the wrist grabs, it is important to try **to ignore the grab**. Getting your attention away from a real danger could be one of the intentions of the assailant. Strike immediately, and then, either execute a release, or keep striking vulnerable points. Remember that even if you hit the opponent on a vulnerable spot and cause him pain, the first instinctive body response will <u>not</u> be to release the grab. Keep striking or execute a strong release technique.

As you are very close, you should also try to neutralize the grabbing hand while you strike, by simply grabbing it, as illustrated [You could use the grab to take the assailant into a Wrist Lock, but this is beyond the scope of beginner's *Krav Maga* that should be kept simple and intuitive under stress].

Lapel Grab: Palm Strike while controlling the grabbing hand

Putting it all together should look like the coming examples. The first set of Drawings illustrates how you immediately palm-strike the opponent's nose (with fingers close to the eyes), while getting hold of the grabbing hand. This should stop any punch or knee on its way to you. Continue with a smoothly-following Forearm Strike to the neck or throat, that becomes a collar/shoulder grab. A Knee Strike to the groin will get him to bend over, so you can hammer-fist the back of his neck or of his head.

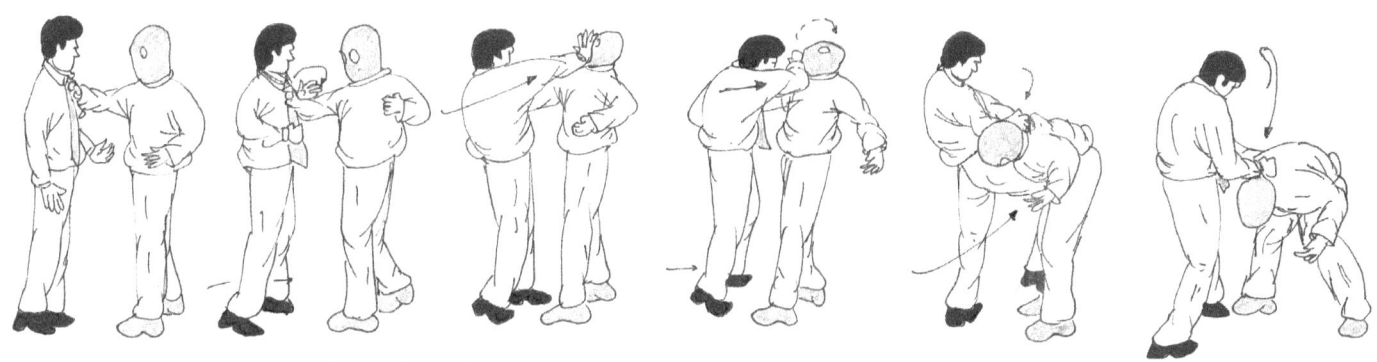

Palm Strike and Hand Grab, Forearm Strike, Groin Knee, Hammer-fist Strike

The second set of Illustrations, coming at the top of next page, shows how to execute a release from the grab, after the first preventive strike: use the hand on the grabbed side to strike his eyes <u>over</u> his grabbing arm. Retract your hand by executing a Downward Elbow Strike into his elbow joint, and follow up with a hip-powered Palm Strike to the nose. Your Hip Twist can naturally turn into a short Roundhouse Kick to the groin. A nice *Retzev* could start with a hip-powered Circular Elbow Strike to the side of the head and a Hammer-fist Strike to the groin.

DEFENSES AGAINST GRABS

Eye Poke, Elbow Joint Strike, Palm Strike, Groin Kick, Elbow Strike, Groin Punch

And we shall complete this section with the similar handling of a **double shirt grab**. In this case, you should worry about a knee to the groin or a head-butt, particularly dangerous if you are pushed or pulled off-balance. Again, an immediate reaction is required.

In the example illustrated below, you strike the opponent's face in the area of the eyes *over* the grabbing arms. Act fast and directly towards the eyes to prevent any attack. You can now retract the hands with a Double Downward Elbow Strike onto the grabbing forearms. Give it all you have: you have to make it painful. Follow up by slapping his ears forcefully in order to grab his head, for a Headbutt on the nose. Pull down on his head while continuing with a Groin Kick. The kicking foot will rebound on the floor for a Knee Strike to the face, face simultaneously pushed down by your hands.

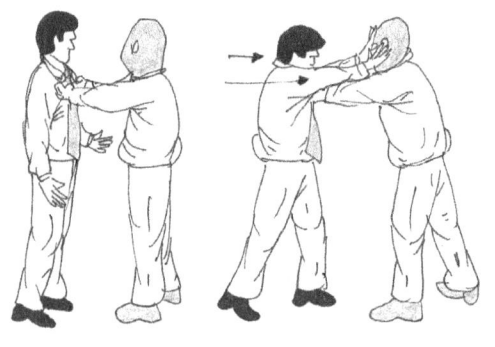

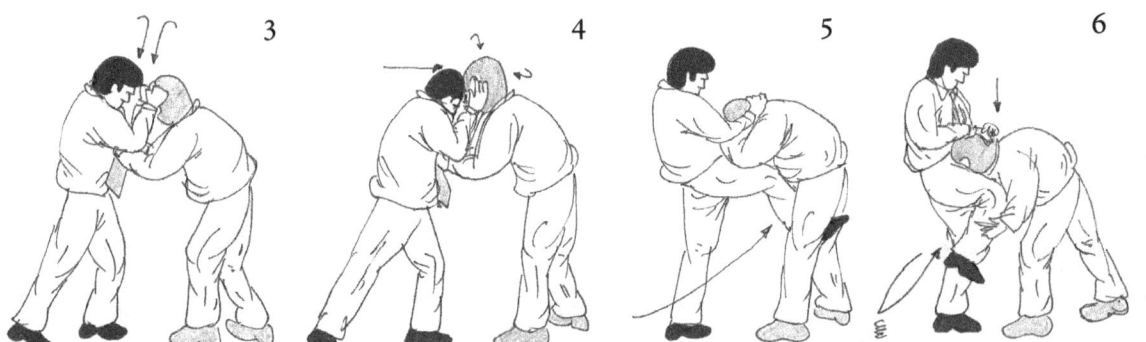

Double Eye Poke, Double Elbow Joint Strike, Double Ear Slap, Headbutt, Groin Kick, Knee to the face

162 KRAV MAGA KICKS

We shall now conclude with a close parent of the lapel grab: *a collar grab from behind*. Whether the assailant pushes or pulls you, the first reaction should be the same: get hold of your lapels and pull strongly down in order to *lock* his fingers into your collar. Do not resist the push or the pull: yield to surprise him, and twist your head brusquely under his grip to face him while painfully locking his fingers. Take hold of his twisted arm to keep it in Arm-lock position, and kick him in the face. Kick through! Start your *Retzev*, for example with a 'Low Kick' to the knee joint.

Lock the assailant fingers with your collar, twist and kick!

5.3 Hair Grab

When someone **grabs your hair**, it is an escalation over grabbing a wrist or a lapel: not only is he invading your personal space and restricting your freedom of movement, but he is also causing you pain. This is an aggression *per se* that justifies the strongest response possible. Needless to remind the reader that it is probably the dangerous prelude to a kick, a punch or a takedown. The reaction must be immediate and the following *Retzev* must be merciless: when your hair is grabbed, you are already under serious attack.

The Photos at the top of next page illustrate the classic Release Technique: Get hold of the grabbing hand with both hands and press firmly (*crush*) the grabbing fingers into your skull. This has the effect of (1) alleviating the pain slightly, of (2) achieving a strong hold and of (3) causing some pain to the aggressor. Nearly simultaneously, you should be kicking his groin. While you lower the kicking foot, you bend down **violently** at the waist and lower your head *as abruptly as possible*. As you hold his grabbing hand firmly, this causes a painful Wrist-lock, and the release of his grip. You can then kick him in the face and/or compound the Wrist-lock with an inside twist of the wrist (See illustrations). Start your own *Retzev* from then on.

Crush the grabbing hand into your skull, kick the groin, bend violently to hurt the wrist joint, follow up

Wrist-locks, in basic *Krav Maga*, are not restraining techniques: they are not locks *per se*. The wrist-lock presented is to be used to hurt the joint and bring the opponent down. These locks in *Krav Maga* are not executed gradually, but **brusquely and violently** to shock the articulation. In the technique above, there are 2 Wrist-lock techniques used, and both must be seen as joint destructions and <u>not</u> control techniques like in *Aikido*. The first Wrist attack is when you immobilize his hand on your skull and violently lower your head. The upward angle of the wrist joint will be jolted from 180 degrees to (much) less than 80 (See Illustration).

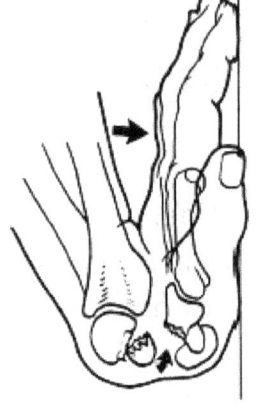

The effect of the bending over his wrist

Once you have freed the hand with the first Joint shock, you twist it to its in-side and press back in what is the *Ni-kyo* wrist-lock of *Aikido*. You push back the hand towards the forearm, and so diminish the downward angle of the wrist joint. The Illustrations show the classic wristlock, to be executed *fast and violently*. This will cause the opponent's fingers to open. One way to use this position to finish the fight is presented further down: lift the wrist up in order to push it back down and out, forcefully. You push down but close to his shoulder joint for a wrist/elbow/shoulder lock that will force him to fall down. Do this forcefully to damage the joints and ensure the takedown. As he lands down, you can stomp his head, armpit, and more.

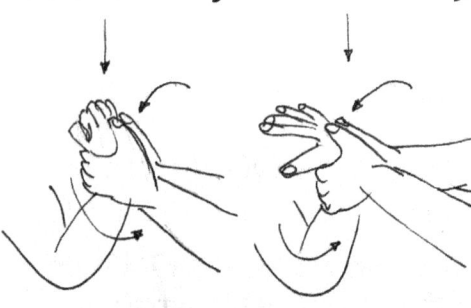

Classic Ni-kyo Wrist-lock

KRAV MAGA KICKS

Wrist-lock Takedown and Stomp

We shall conclude this section with a defense against a **hair grab from behind**. You do not know what the assailant has in store for you and you do not have the luxury to grab his hand and crush it into a wrist-lock. The best way to handle this situation is to surprise the attacker by jumping towards him while twisting. He expects you to resist, but, instead, you go with the flow and throw yourself at him. Twist and aim at *headbutting* him (with the side of the skull, as illustrated. Keep your momentum to crowd him and palm-strike his groin. You also use the other hand to catch his grabbing wrist from the outside and to remove his grab. The hand that struck his groin now goes up to poke his eyes. You can see from the Drawings below that your knee is in perfect position for a Knee Strike to the groin. Keep at it...

If your hair is pulled from behind, surprise the assailant by throwing yourself at him; start hitting immediately: headbutt, groin strike, eye poke and groin knee

DEFENSES AGAINST GRABS

6. Defenses against Holds

6.1 Bear Hug from the Front

A Bear Hug from the front is a serious close combat attack. If you get caught, it means you have let your guard down and let an assailant much too close. You should keep your distance and always stop-strike anyone breaching your safety zone. Be aware of your surroundings, trust your gut and use preemptive strikes: this should help you avoid ending up in a *bear hug*.
There are two main types of Front Bear Hugs: your hands are either **free** <u>or</u> **caught under the hug**.

a.   <u>Hands-free Bear Hug from the Front</u>

Being caught in a **Bear Hug with your hands free** is not the worse of situations. As you will see, your hands will cause him serious damage fast, while his hands are neutralized by the Hold. So, why would someone want to take you in such a hug? *First*, he could be stupid. *Second*, beware of a possible incoming headbutt and/or groin Knee Strike: place your head besides his and squeeze your upper thighs in. *Third*, he could be very strong and try to painfully squeeze your chest or lower ribs before forcing you to the ground. But *Fourth* and most probably, it is the beginning of a Takedown, like what is illustrated in the coming sets of Drawings. Therefore, you need to act fast...

Outer Leg Block Takedown from a Front Bear Hug

Suplex-like Sacrifice Takedown from a Front Bear Hug

The best approach is an early reaction before the assailant can fully set the Bear Hug. If you have not been able to offensively preempt the attack, and have let him get too close, you can still react as he dives to lock his hands in your back. The coming Illustrations show how to catch his head with both hands, make a large step rearwards, lower your center of gravity and deflect his forward attack momentum. Try to catch the head with forcefully, and with your fingers near or in his *eyes*. You then invert the direction of your reaction and pivot in the other direction: use your hips and body to pull his head in a downward spiral to the other side, all the way to the floor. Your fingers in his eyes will do much to help the takedown. Stomp him as he reaches the floor.

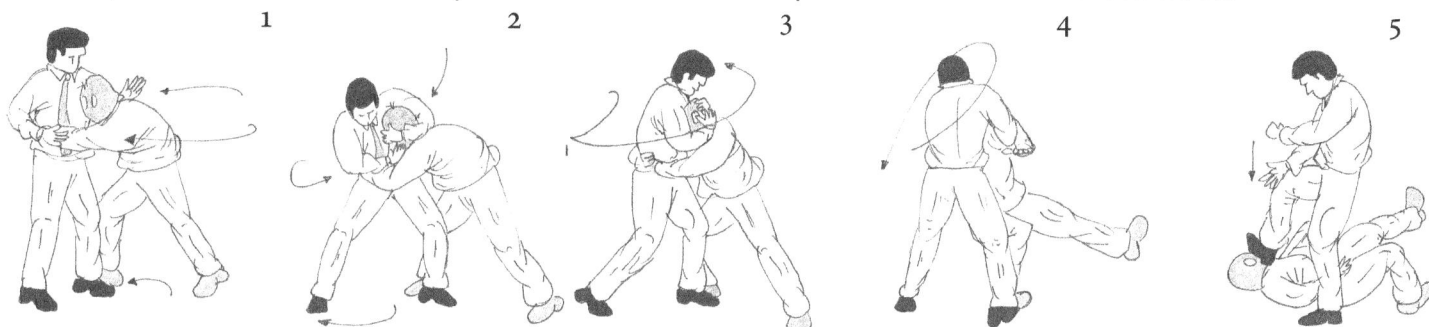

If the Hug is not set, pull away while grabbing his head for a Head Twisting Takedown

If you have been **caught in the hug**, the following Photos illustrate one way to deal with the attacker. It is pretty simple: Immediately *slap his ears* forcefully, knee his groin and push him away. Follow him with a Front Kick to the groin, hopping if necessary to cover the distance. Keep the *Retzev* on with an Eye Whip and a Low Kick to the knee. Note that you can also headbutt his nose after the Twin Ear Slap, if this is something that is up your alley. When you slap his ears, you should strike as if you want your hands to meet in the middle of his head, and with the palms over the ears. This will cause a brain shock, an eardrum tear, a loss of balance and a searing pain.

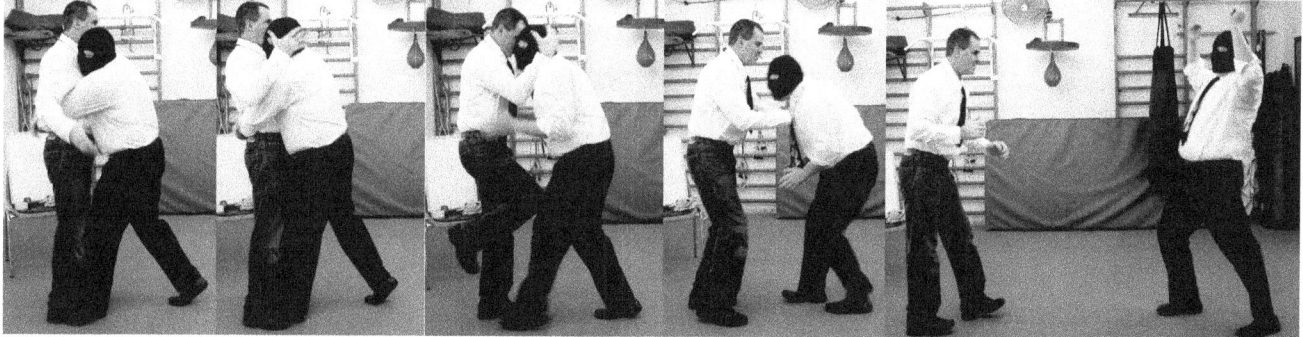

Slap his ears as soon as he claps on the Hug, and start a merciless Retzev

DEFENSES AGAINST HOLDS

Here comes what to do **once the hold is well set**, or if it is a very serious situation (like more than one attacker or a threat of permanent bodily harm). Press his eye balls with your thumbs and push his head back and down. Your hands hold and press his head at cheekbones level while applying pressure on the eyes, and you step deep behind his own legs. Apply just enough pressure to the eyes to force his head down to the floor with your hands. If necessary, slam his head on the floor before straightening back up for a Stomp or two on his ankle joints. [<u>**CAUTION: This is an extremely dangerous technique, potentially crippling and even lethal. Drill with utmost control and use carefully and ethically only in a life-threatening situation**</u>.]

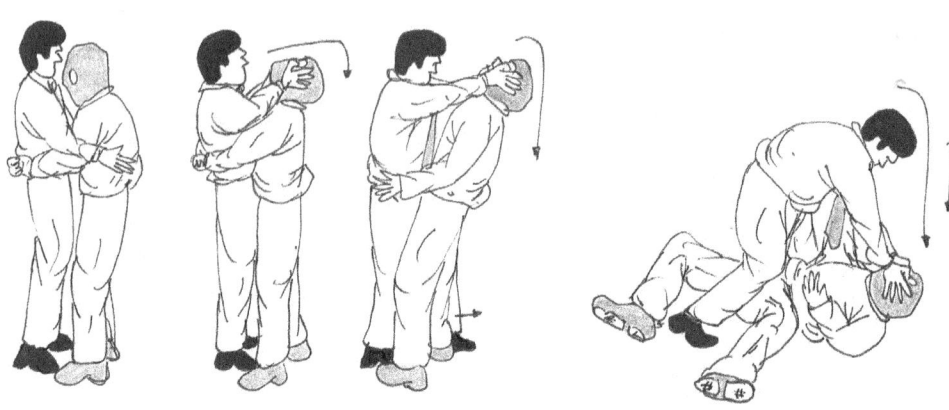

In very serious situations, simply press his eyeballs with both thumbs

A similar but **slightly milder** way to deal with the hugging attack is presented in the Drawings below. Instead of pressing the eyeballs, you will *press up the cartilage below his nose* and push his head back and then down. Use both your hands and place them on and below his nose, with one finger joint on the upper lip just below the nose. Push the cartilage violently up to force his head back. If you try to do that by pushing his chin, he will be able to resist by using his neck muscles; pressing the nose up solves this problem. Use both hands and the fingers under the nose to push his head back and down (in an arc) until he releases his hold. You then grab his ear or his hair with one hand, while keeping the pressure under the nose with the other. Twist his head down all the way to the floor, and Palm Strike it to slam it, again, into the ground.

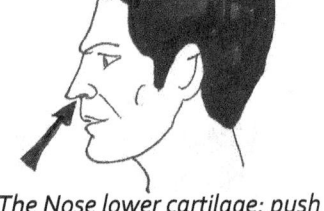

The Nose lower cartilage: push diagonally up

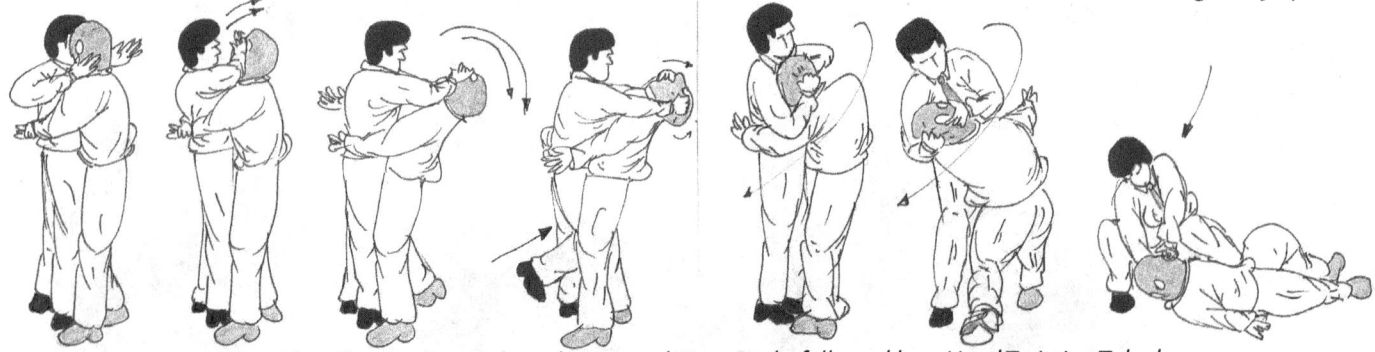

Less potentially crippling: Release by Upward Nose Push, followed by a Head Twisting Takedown

b. Hands-caught Bear hug from the Front

If your **arms are caught under the bear hug**, you are in the same danger as before: he could be waiting for an accomplice, he could be already kneeing you or head-butting you, or he is planning the same kind of Takedown that we have presented before. But, this time, *you do not have your hands free for a fast and crippling reaction*. His hands are not free, but neither are yours. You should have preempted this one...
React as fast and as early as possible, place your head outside his in order to avoid a headbutt, and strive to keep your testicles safe.

If you can react before he claps on the hold, go back with your hips and slap his groin with both hands. If you have little room for maneuver, slap as much as you can **and grab**. That should stop the attempted hold. You have pulled back the hips for protection and to make room for the groin slap. You can now use the range created for a Groin Kick. Lift and open your arms to fully free them and hammer-fist the back of his neck presented, as he bends in pain. Keep his face down and knee it. See Drawings below.

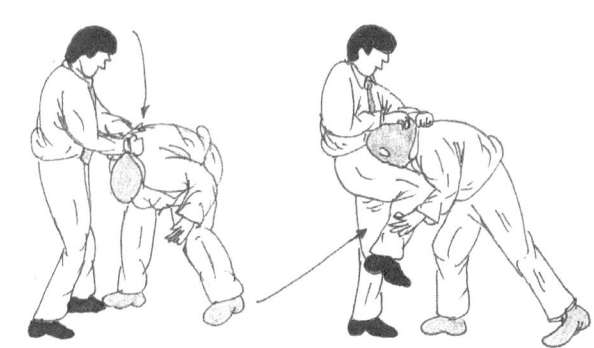

React as soon as possible: pull your hips back and slap his groin

If the assailant has already secured a strong hold, **stomp** his foot immediately. Strike with the heel, *all the way through, and target the toes or the ankle*. The purpose of the stomp is (1) to interrupt the attacker's plan, (2) to inflict pain and (3) to create a diversion. Use the reaction to the Stomp to slide your hands in between the two bodies and **grab his groin** forcefully. As he instinctively pulls his hips, knee his groin and lift your arms to create some space. Pull one arm out of his grip and immediately place the thumb of the freed hand on his ocular globe, as illustrated at the top of next page (*on an unmasked opponent*). You could bring him down with pressure on the eye(s) like in the previous section, but we propose another finish here. You'll instinctively use what goes best for you. *After thumbing his eye to obtain full release, you can catch his trachea*. You can place the other hand on his face near the eyes as well. Squeeze his trachea while pushing it back and down. You step simultaneously deep forward and move the other hand to his lower back (to help 'break' his posture). **Keep the trachea squeeze all the way down** and slam his head into the ground.

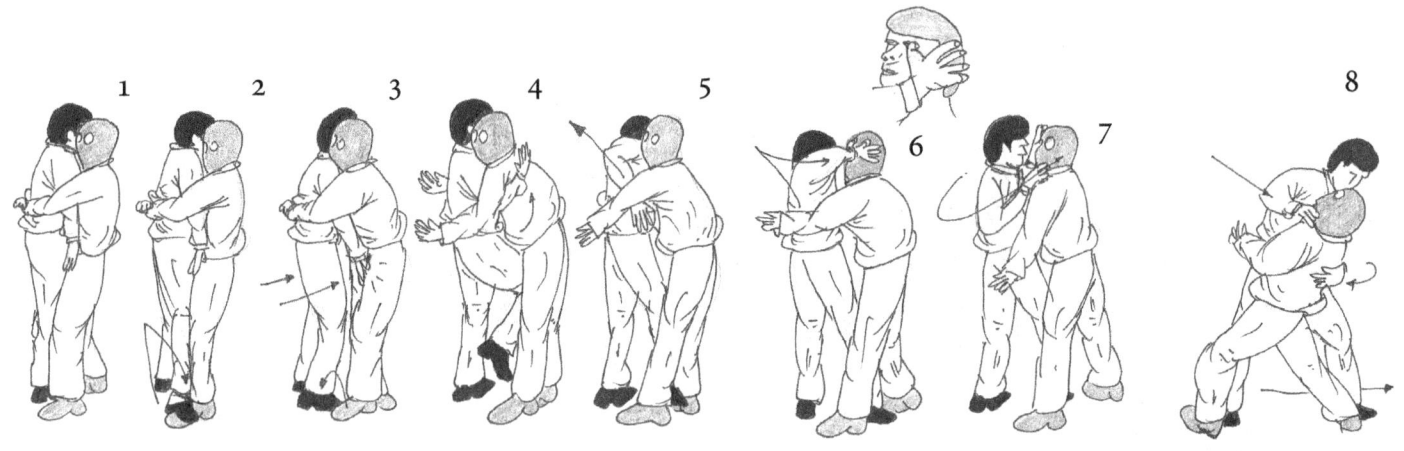

Stomp his foot to allow for slipping your hands towards his groin; then thumb his eye and follow up

To conclude this section, we shall present a set of Drawings illustrating what to do if you are caught in a Front Bear Hug **and immediately lifted off your feet.** This is probably the prelude to slamming you down. You should *immediately hook one foot behind his leg*, from the outside; try to hook into the back of the knee, to avoid being lifted higher and to 'root' you for the coming Knee Strike. You other leg has in fact been taking some range for a Knee Strike to his groin as powerful as possible. Use the commotion to pull out one arm and thumb his eye. From there you can start your own Retzev, based on those of this and the previous section…

If lifted in a Front Bear Hug, hook behind one of his legs and knee his groin, before thumbing his eye

6.2 Bear Hug from the Back

One cannot be blamed for having been caught in a Bear Hug from the back. One should always be vigilant and aware of his surroundings, but an aggressor has the advantage of planning, of surprise and of taking the initiative. Still, trust your gut if your 6th sense gives you a weird feeling of unease, and increase vigilance. Do not hesitate to change path, to stop or retrace your steps if anything looks wrong: there is no shame in it, whatsoever.
All this is to remind the reader that preempting a surprise attack from the rear is pretty difficult. Again, immediate reaction is required!
Just like for the previous section, we shall divide this one in the handling of the hands-free and the hands-caught versions of the Hug.

a. Hands-free Bear Hug from the Back

We shall start by illustrating the way to execute a Bear Hug from the Back, *if we were the attacker*. This is to show that a Bear Hug is a <u>dynamic</u> attack with a purpose, and to underline how important is the immediate reaction. Someone who gets you in a Bear Hug and does nothing is not an experienced fighter, even if he waits for an accomplice, he should be at least shaking you around. The Bear Hug from the Back is simply a Takedown: you slam into the opponent while setting your hold in order to take his center of gravity and to cause him to react by pushing back. As he does, you pull him back and down with your whole body. That's it! Wham Bam! No fiddling around.

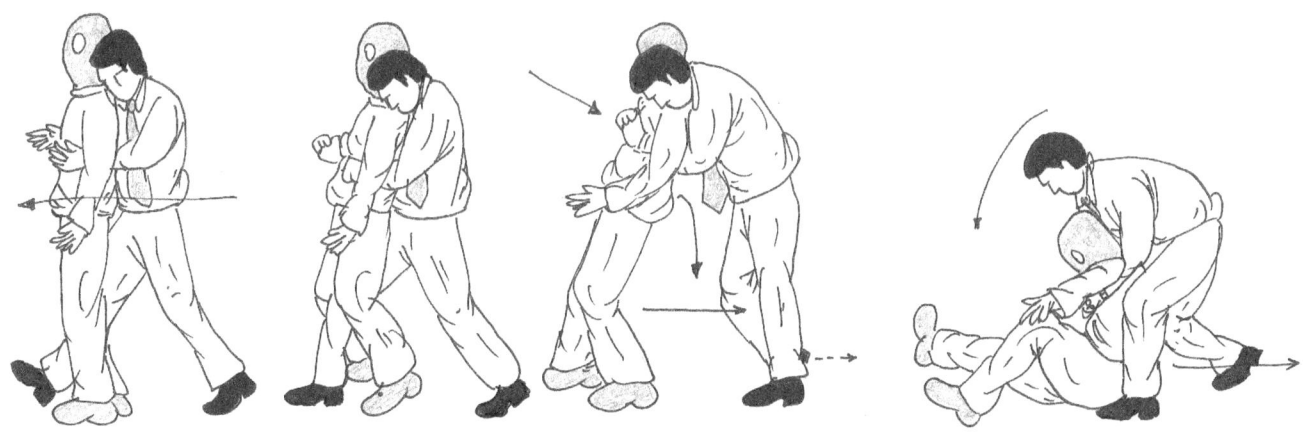

The realistic use of the Rear Bear Hug

If you can react *before the attacker can clinch the hold*, you should react as illustrated by the coming Drawings. Immediately pivot towards the assailant, and step forcefully between his legs while executing a very natural but *hips-powered* Circular Rear Elbow Strike. The step is very important and has the following purposes: (1) to strike his groin area with your upper thigh, (2) to bring you close to his axis (neutralizes the hold), and (3) to power the Elbow Strike. The Elbow Strike must go *through* his head: it is not a contact slap. Follow-up with a naturally-following Circular Front Elbow Strike to the side of his head. Keep the *Retzev* going, for example with a Ghost Groin Kick and another Elbow Strike.

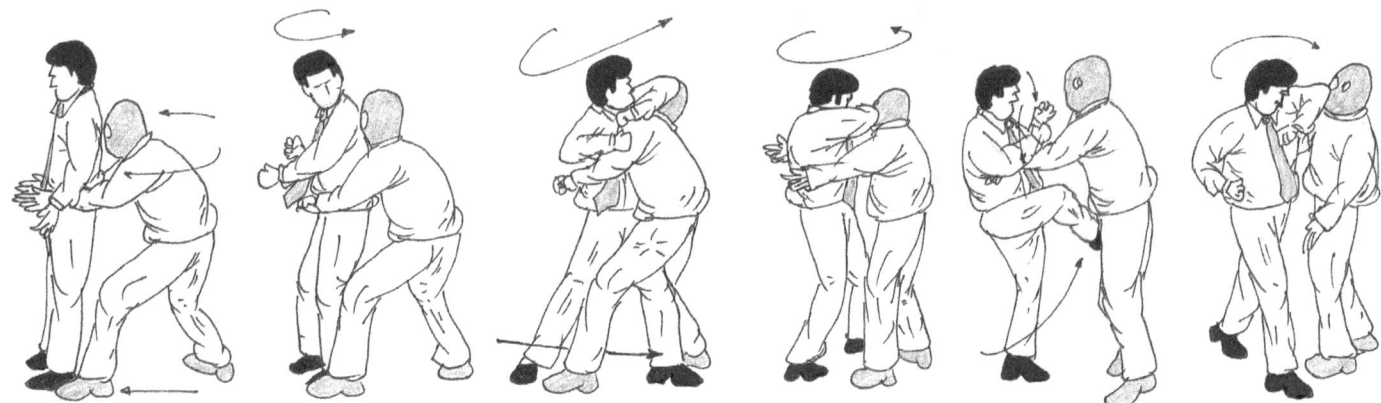

If you detect the attack before the hold is set, pivot immediately and step into him with an Elbow Strike

If you are a good ground-fighter and if you are sure that your assailant is alone, you can try the following technique. It is the 'Sacrifice' version of a classic Takedown, especially suitable for use against this hold. As soon as you detect the attack, clasp his hands so as to not let him go. Pull a leg and bring it behind him together with your hips. You do that *explosively* while letting some of your weight on his grip. Simultaneously, you slap his groin with the close hand. As soon as you are in position, with your lower body behind his legs, let go of the other hand as well and grab the back of both his knees. In order for the maneuver to be effective, you need to have your hips *lower* than his center of gravity and *use them to tip him over*. Lift both his knees as high as possible while straightening the legs and the trunk. Up to this point, we have described the classic *Sukui Nage*-type Takedown as it is usually executed. You simply throw the opponent to the ground from where you have lifted him. We shall illustrate this classic Throw in the next section (hands-caught bear Hug from the Back).
In this example, we shall <u>throw</u> the opponent towards the ground, head first, but we shall accompany him. Fall on top of him as he slams into the floor *for a more damaging fall*. Follow up on the ground. This is a very damaging technique, recommended if the circumstances are suitable (See top of next page). Of course, if you are a mediocre ground-fighter, or if the assailant has accomplices around, just execute the classic standing Takedown.

Crushing Sacrifice Takedown against a Hands-free Bear hug from the Rear

And now, we shall present the *classic* release from the hug **once it has been clinched**. Immediately hit him in the groin area with your buttocks, while bending forward. The bending is to make yourself heavy for a lift or a pull. The *Buttocks Strike* is much more effective than it may seem; just make sure it is explosive and powerful. [If your assailant has started pulling you back, all that must be preceded by a *Rear Head Strike*, hoping that the assailant has not taken the precaution of placing his head besides yours]. As soon as you have hit him with your glutes, use the knuckles of one fist to strike the back of his upper clasping hand. The purpose is to cause pain in order to help your other hand to peel off one of his fingers. *Use all fingers and concentrate on grabbing one finger only.* Do not try to unlock the grasp of his whole hand, one finger is enough and much easier. Once you have his finger, bend it over forcefully and violently. If the Knuckle Strike has not been enough, you should seamlessly stomp one of his feet before proceeding to the finger grab; or you can stomp in any case just to be sure. Pivot towards him and keep the Finger Lock set in your fist. Lift your leg directly into his groin as you now face him, and elbow his head while keeping his finger bent-over. Keep at it if necessary.

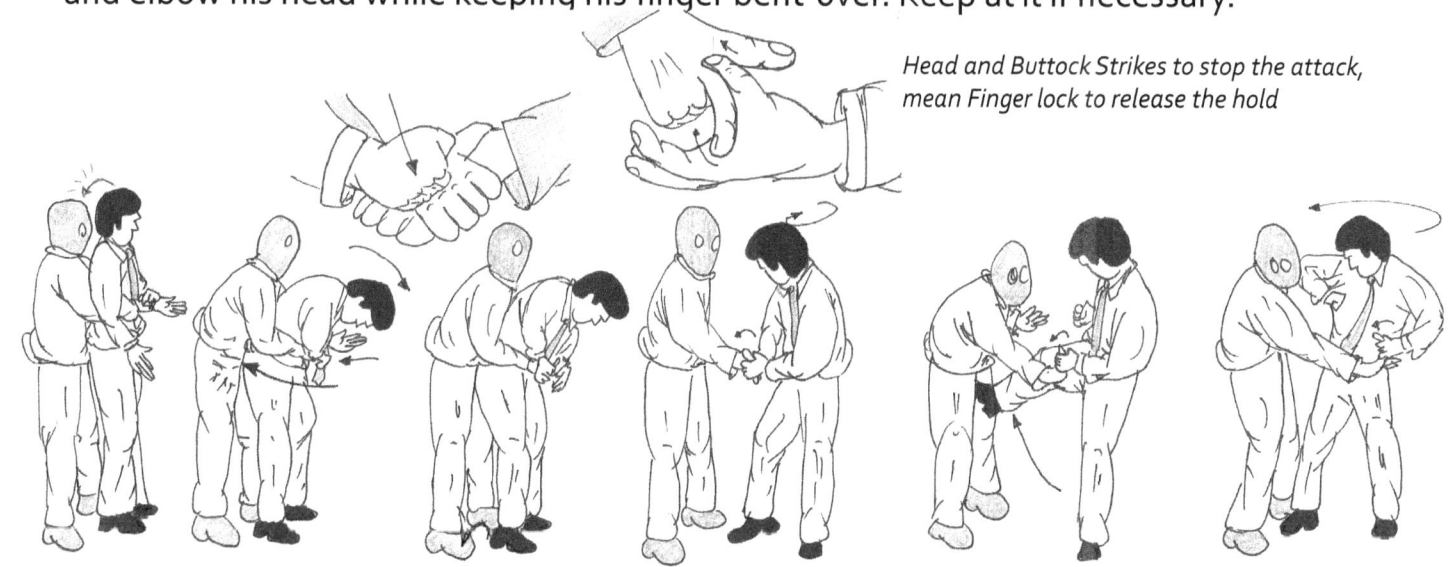

Head and Buttock Strikes to stop the attack, mean Finger lock to release the hold

DEFENSES AGAINST HOLDS

If you are more of a striker, then the '**attrition**' release presented in the coming Photos is better for you. You shall hit him all over until he releases you, and then you can start your following *Retzev*. Start with an immediate Back Headbutt and a foot Stomp. A Hooking Heel Back Kick to the shin should rattle him more. By then he should have pulled back and given you enough space for a Hooking Groin Back Kick. Notice the orthodox delivery: once you have struck into the groin, hook back forward for additional damage. Please note that it could be necessary to alternate the sides you attack if the assailant moves sideways to reaction to your hits.

Keep hitting the attacker with the head and the feet, until he releases you

KRAV MAGA KICKS

b. Hands-caught Bear Hug from the Back

All the principles already covered in Bear Hug defenses stay relevant for this section. **Your arms are now caught under the hold** and you will be able to release them only after adequate 'softening' of the assailant. The best method to release the weakened hold is presented in the coming two sets of Photos: you twist the arms in order to place the back of your hands together and then you lift them violently while straightening them. The *first* set of Photos is a simple 'Release and elbow'.

The *second* example is the release followed by the standing version of the *Double Leg Lift Takedown* already encountered above. Note that, unless executed very early in the hugging attempt, both series should be preceded by 'softening' strikes and followed by an aggressive *Retzev*.

The arms-release technique and a Back Elbow Strike to the solar plexus

The release leading to the Double Leg lift Takedown

DEFENSES AGAINST HOLDS

Once this is acquired, let us see how to *fully* handle the attack.

The Illustrations below show how to react if you have detected the attack and can start your defense **before the assailant can clasp hands**: immediately lift your forearms and step aside. This will give you room for a Hand Strike to the *groin* (Palm or Knife-hand). From the Groin Strike, you directly lift the elbow into his face (that is coming down). Both strikes, to the groin and to the face are powerful 'strike-through' hits. From there, you'll start your follow-up series; for example: a Hooking Upward Back Kick to the groin, another Elbow Strike to the face and a Stomping Side kick to the side of his knee.

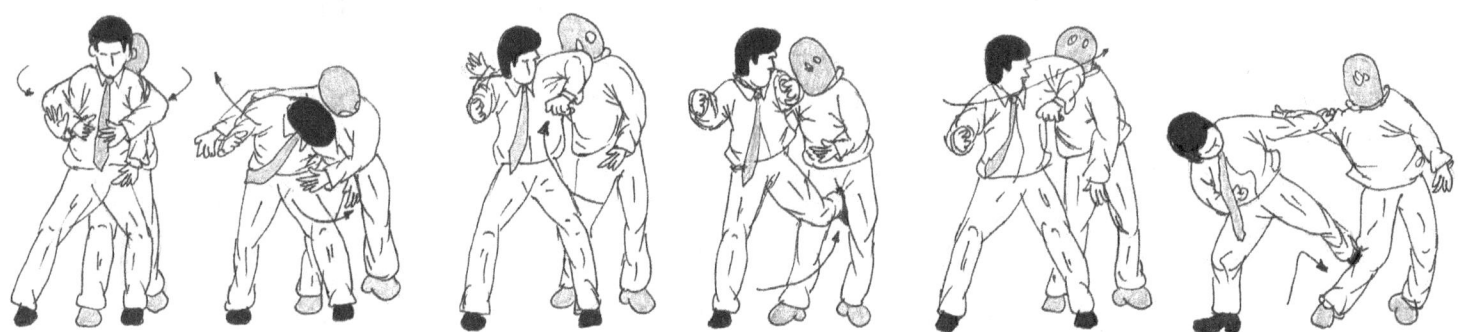

If you can react to the hugging early enough, step aside to hit his groin with your hand

Once the Bear Hug is set, it is better to adopt an *attrition* strategy: strike the assailant until his hold weakens and then execute the release described at the beginning of the section. We shall present a possible series of strikes, but it will in fact depend on your affinities and on the reactions of the attacker. There are a few principles to respect: (1) strike through and explosively, (2) alternate the height of your strikes to overwhelm him and prevent his initiatives, and (3) alternate sides you use to strike. If you slap his groin with your left hand or stomp his left foot, it is highly probable that he will move to the right, instinctively and to avoid further hits. You have then to make use of his reaction and to hit him from your right side, to the groin or lower legs that he is moving there. It is pretty simple but requires training and drilling.

In the example illustrated at the top of next page, you *headbutt* his nose as soon as he clasps over your arms. Immediately move slightly sideways to hit (or grab) his *groin* with your hand. Follow up with Donkey Back Kicks to the shin, Stomps, more Hand-strikes to the groin. You can execute a Hooking Upward Back Kick on one side after having hand-struck him in the groin from the other side to cause him to move. This should have weakened his hold and given you enough room to execute the release. Strike his head with the elbow of one arm being released, follow up with another Elbow Strike and a Groin Kick.

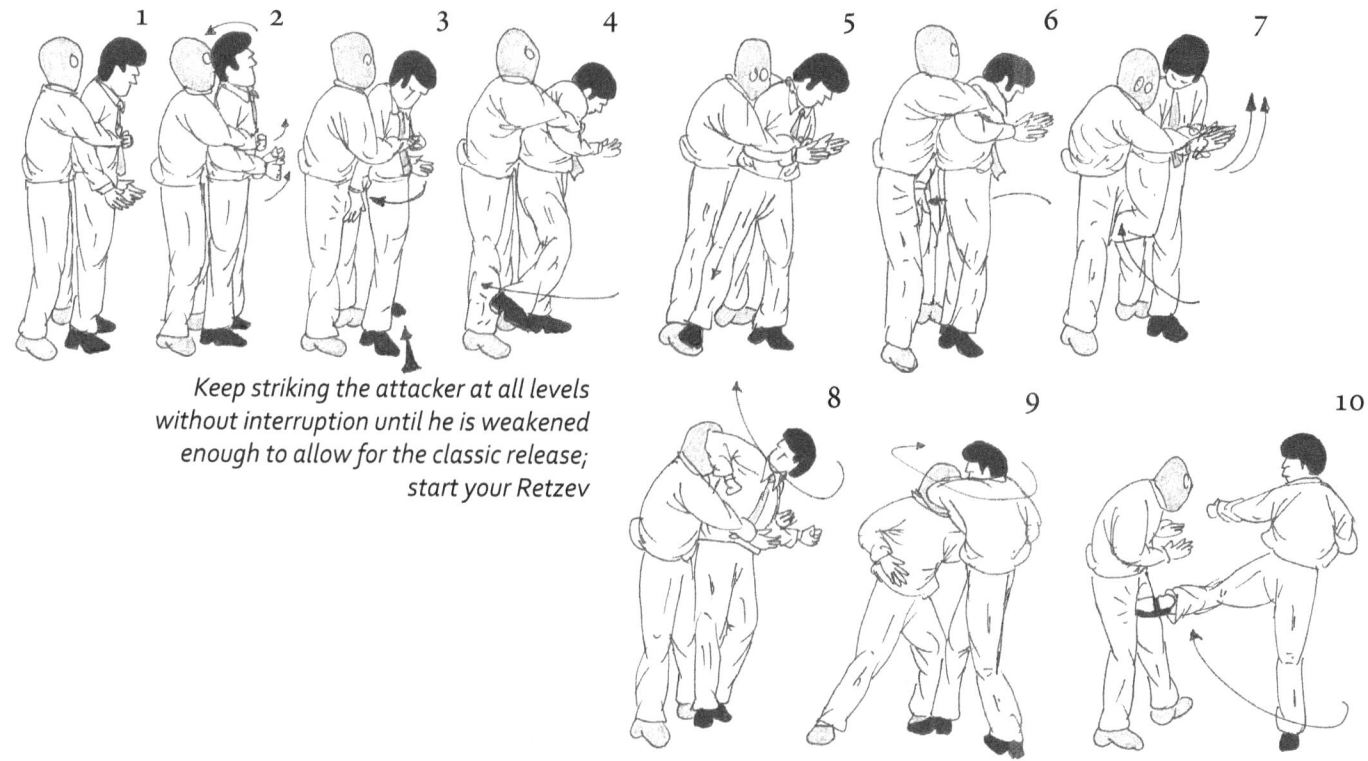

Keep striking the attacker at all levels without interruption until he is weakened enough to allow for the classic release; start your Retzev

We shall conclude this section by dealing, again, with the case in which the assailant **starts to lift you up immediately as he sets the hold**. Needless to mention that you'll be slammed to the floor if you do not react at once. You should hook behind his leg with one leg, to avoid being lifted too high, and you simultaneously kick his groin with the other in *Hooking Donkey Back Kick style.* Kick hard and into the groin, with everything you have got. You should then join your hands for the classic release while you land back down. Follow up with any of the grounded techniques presented above according to the circumstances. We have illustrated here a Knife-hand Strike to the groin. Keep the *Retzev* going.

If lifted in rear Bear Hug, hook one leg behind his and hook the other heel forcefully into his groin

Do not fear going forward slowly; fear only to stand still.
~Chinese Proverb

6.3 Side Headlock

A Side headlock is a very bad situation to find yourself in. You should react early to avoid the lock, and we shall give a few examples. If caught, react immediately and violently, because an experienced opponent will not linger but take you the ground and/or twist your vertebrae in a very dangerous Neck-lock. He could also release one hand to punch you in the still immobilized face. And remember that your assailant could have an accomplice around…

So the best approach is, again, offensive preemption. If it is becoming clear that somebody is about to attack you, forget your social graces and stop him in his tracks. This is even truer if a potential assailant comes too close for comfort, even if he is not attacking yet. Do not let your polite and considerate upbringing stop you from reacting just because the other guy is sweet-talking you. The sets of Photos below illustrate a few possible reactions to someone coming from the side and placing his arm on your shoulders or around your neck. Female readers can easily identify with such an aggression: touching you or invading your personal space is an aggression and can lead to much more than that. Do not tolerate it!

In the first example, you simply side-elbow the *nose* (center of the face) of the attacker; in the second example, you take him down with a Tilting Hip Throw; and in the third you stomp-side-kick his knee.

React early and elbow the face of the assailant,…

…or take him down over your upper thighs

...or crush his side knee to the ground

The next step is to try to react **before the assailant can clasp the lock shut**. The set of Illustrations below shows how to catch the hand of the opponent (the one going over your neck). In that case, you should not resist the downward pressure, but go with it until you have a firm grab. You then go down and rearwards to evade the lock while twisting his arm in a classic Armlock. Remember that, in basic *Krav Maga*, an Arm-lock is an attack executed violently: twist brusquely and strike his elbow with force. Kick his face as he is driven down by the lock. You can then keep at it, for example by twisting his arm in his back and then pushing him down and forward with the locked arms and with your hips.

Grab the hand encircling your neck before it can clasp and evade into a classic Arm-lock

DEFENSES AGAINST HOLDS

Once the Lock is set, the situation requires hitting vulnerable points in order to weaken the assailant's hold. You have two options, and the good news is that it will be difficult for the opponent to guard both targets simultaneously. The first target is the **groin**, like usual, that can be struck and/or grabbed with your outer hand, as will be illustrated a few times in the coming full Releases. The other general target is the **head**, that can be reached with your inner hand; you should aim at striking and pressing the *eyes* or the *throat*. You should try to strike both areas when possible, but can start drilling as illustrated by the Photos.

Drill attacking the throat, then push it down to release the hold; Keep striking, preferably the throat or the groin

If the confrontation is serious, attacking the eyes is better than attacking the throat

Now, **let us put it all together** in the following set of Drawings. When head-locked, slap his *groin* immediately. Then grab it while going for the eyes with the other hand. Push his head back by pressing his *eyeballs*, and use the 'groin hand' to lift the leg close to you. Lift as high as possible while pushing his head down. As he releases your neck, try to keep control of his arm. Once he is on the ground, pull his arm up while stomp-kicking his floating ribs.

Slap-grab the groin, rake/press the eyes, take him down and stomp his ribs

KRAV MAGA KICKS

Another way to finish the release, after the groin and eyes attack, is presented here. Immediately strike and grab his groin and go for the eyes. Twist the grabbed testicles while pressing on the eyeballs until he releases the lock. Push his head back by pressing the eyes, in order to uncover his throat. Strike the throat with a Knife-hand or a Hammer-fist Strike and kick his groin while pushing him back all the way to the floor.

Another redoubtable finish to the classic release

In some cases, the opponent locks your neck and immediately starts twisting with the probable purpose of **taking you to the ground**. Slap his groin. But, in that case, you should not resist, or better you should give him a spike of resistance in order to cause him to push down even more forcefully. Then, following the principle of letting him slam the unlocked door, you throw yourself to the floor while twisting. By surprising him so you get control of going to the ground and you get helped by his own push. And do not forget to keep your slapping 'groin hand' grabbing his testicles; that will definitely help! After a full Roll, you should end up over him. If he has not released you yet, let your 'grabbing' hand let go but come back at once to hit the groin again. Your other forearm his slamming into the side of his head, and you rake his eyes as you lift the arm back. The 'groin' hand grabs his *fingers* and the 'eyes' hand pushes his elbow forward as you pull your head out. See Illustrations at the top of next page.

DEFENSES AGAINST HOLDS

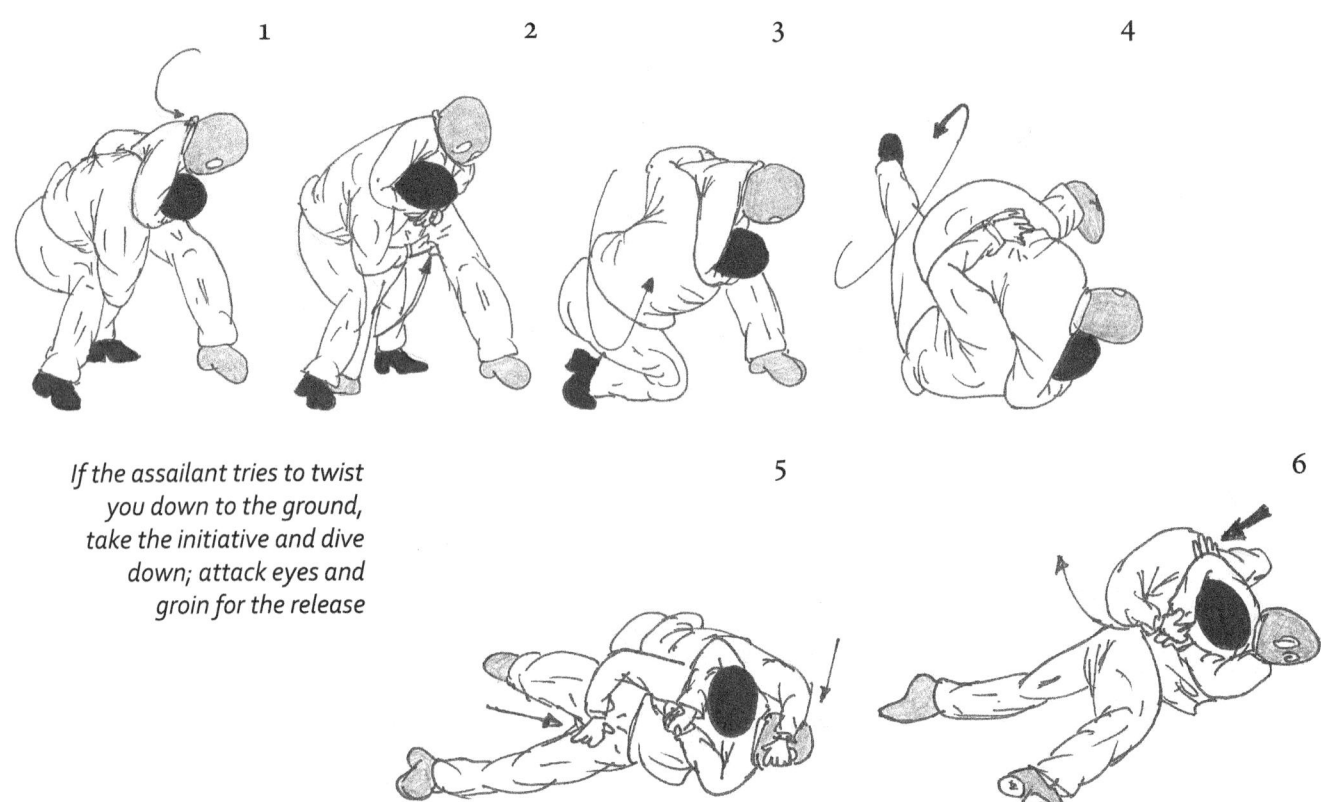

If the assailant tries to twist you down to the ground, take the initiative and dive down; attack eyes and groin for the release

7. Defenses against Chokes

Make no mistake, a **choke** is a lethal attack and should be treated as such. It is as dangerous as being threatened with a knife. It is fiendishly easy to crush a larynx, to permanently damage a trachea, to cut blood flow to the brain or to asphyxiate someone. And it can happen very fast.

Therefore, let me repeat: act as early as possible and go for the most vulnerable targets. At once!

7.1 Hands Choke from the Front

The typical **Hand Choke from the front** would not be used by a trained opponent, but it does not mean that it is not dangerous. It is a *Respiratory Choke*, painfully cutting your oxygen intake, and also potentially damaging to the physical integrity of the larynx. React fast because the lack of oxygen will very quickly hamper your strength and your speed.

If you cannot act **preemptively** as the assailant approaches, you should at least be ready to strike *before he starts squeezing*.

<u>All the release techniques that we shall present in this section should be preceded by a 'stopping' maneuver that will at least slow the setting of the grip and rattle your opponent</u>. It can be a simple Poke to the eyes, a Poke to the throat or a Ghost Kick to the groin (illustrated in the coming Drawings). Remember that, in a high adrenalin situation, this will not necessarily stop your opponent, but it will allow you to proceed with the release techniques in better conditions.

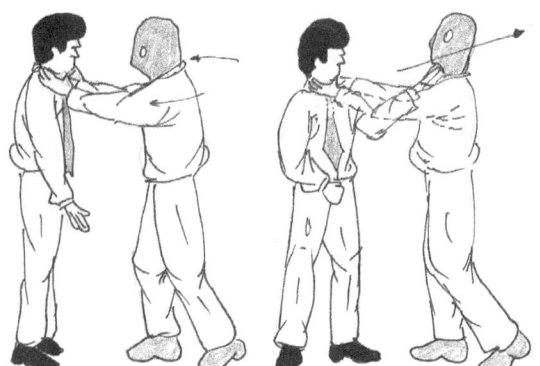

Strike the assailant's throat with your straightened fingertips or with the first knuckles; note that the left arm of the victim has not been drawn for clarity of the stop-poke,

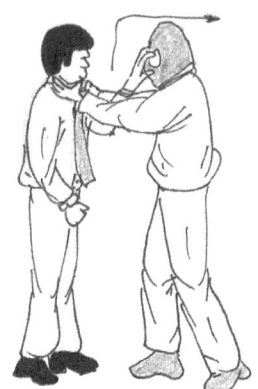

...or claw into his eyes as soon as possible in the attack,

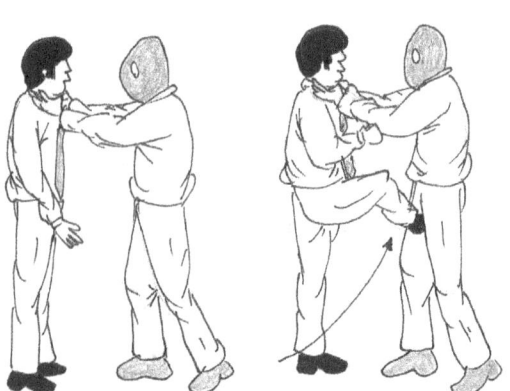

...or lift your foot directly into his testicles, in a Front Ghost Groin Kick.

Once this has been made clear, we can now present the release techniques. The *best* reactive technique is, in the author's opinion, the one we shall present first. The following Photos illustrate how you must first lower your chin, lift your shoulders and contract your neck muscles to relieve the pressure. You then lift one arm immediately, straight up and twist your upper body *violently* in the direction of the other arm. While twisting, you start a powerful *Downward Elbow Strike onto the choking arms* of the attacker. That will release the hold and place you in perfect position for a horizontal Side Elbow Strike to the face (Aim for the nose). Remember that the maneuver will work best after a destabilizing strike, and that it must be followed by a serious *Retzev* until total victory.

The best release: lift arm, twist, elbow down, side-elbow to counter

The keys for the success of the Release technique are (1) to lift the arm *high* in order to immobilize the choking hand between the shoulder and the neck, (2) to *twist violently* with 'seriously damaging his wrist' in mind, and (3) to *elbow down as an attack* of the joints and not as a release. The coming Illustrations try to show the amount of energy and commitment needed for this maneuver.

Lift the arm and twist violently, elbow down and through with everything you have, twist back with the hips for the Elbow counter

Let us now put it all together with the stopping strike and some follow-up. In the Drawings below, you can see how to go back with the momentum of the assault while tucking the chin and lifting the shoulders. You attack the eyes while lifting the other arm. Pivot violently and elbow down, whether he has already released the choke or not. Come back up with a Forearm Strike to the side of the neck. Kick his groin and follow with an Elbow Strike.

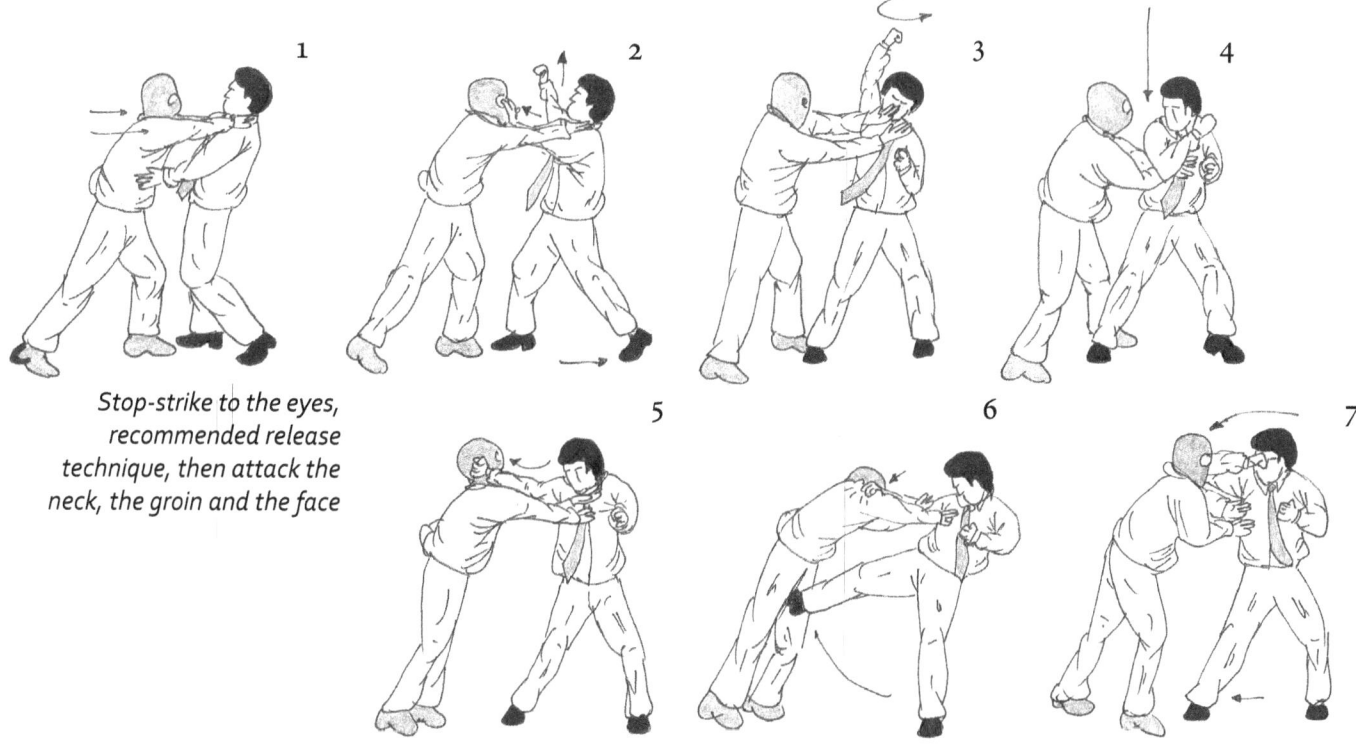

Stop-strike to the eyes, recommended release technique, then attack the neck, the groin and the face

DEFENSES AGAINST CHOKES

The next set of Illustrations shows the same release technique, but when backed against the wall and with a different preventive stop-strike and simultaneous kicking techniques (See 'Low Kicks').

Ghost Stop Kick to the groin, followed by the release technique with simultaneous Knee Kick with Shin Grating to Foot Stomp

The general Release Technique presented above, is, -in the eyes of the author-, the best and the most versatile. But there are other release maneuvers available, and some could be more adapted to the circumstances and to the personality of the trainee. **Just remember** the *preceding Stop-strike* and the *Retzev*.

<u>The first possibility</u> is illustrated in the next Photos and Drawings: it is the '**breaking**' of the hold **by hitting the grabbing arms forcefully <u>upward</u>s**. You concentrate your power by joining the hands or the fists, and you bend the knees to go slightly down as you strike up. Remember NOT to intertwine the fingers: it is dangerous for the joints.

Place your palms strongly together and strike both up and out, slap both of his ears, catch the head and knee the face

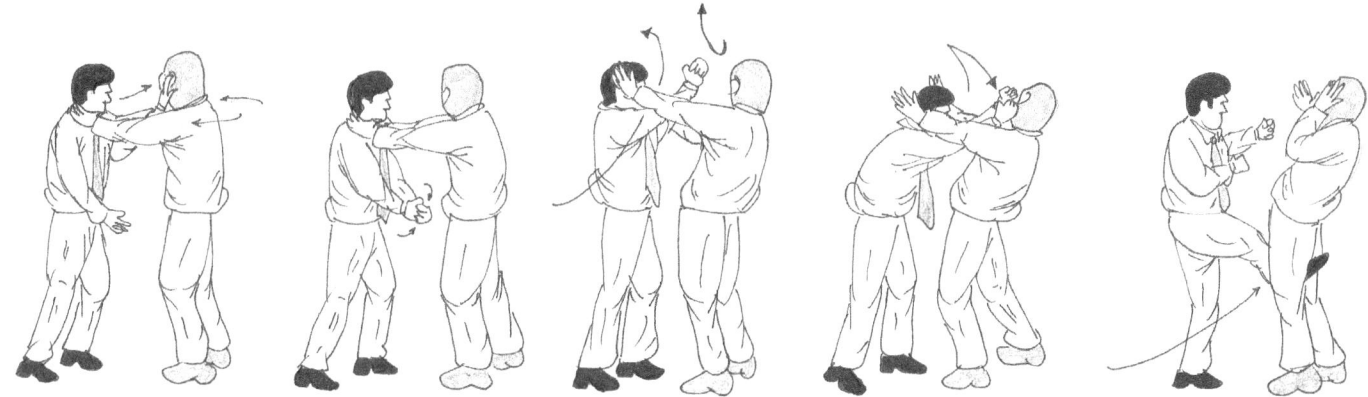
Join the fists and strike up forcefully, come back down on his nose and kick his groin

Another release method will have you striking <u>down</u> on the grabbing hands, *with everything you have*. Use the Knife side of the hand and the forearms to strike *through with your whole body*. You should aim for the fleshy part of the upper forearm of the attacker, close to the elbow; this part is rich in nerve endings. Open the arms after crashing through. Follow up with a Groin Kick and then with an Elbow Strike down into the exposed back of his neck.

Striking down on the choking arms and follow-up

Sometimes **simplicity** is best, especially if you can start your technique *very early* in the grabbing. The next technique is a simplified version of our preferred Release Maneuver, also advisable if you are stronger than the attacker, and/or he has not strengthened his grip yet. You simply use a Knife-hand arm movement *through* the hold and come back with a Knife-hand Strike to the neck or throat.

A simple and easy version of the preferred release technique

DEFENSES AGAINST CHOKES

And we shall conclude with a last set of Photos putting it all together: a Ghost Groin Kick as a stopping strike, an upward-arms-strike Release, a Knife-hand Strike, Low Kick and Elbow finish.

Ghost Groin Kick stopping strike and Upward Strike Release; follow-up

Quality is not an act, it is a habit.
~Aristotle

7.2 Hands Choke from the Back

A hands-choke from the rear will not allow you a preemptive strike; neither will it be easy to use a stopping strike before your release technique. But, on the other hand, it is not the most dangerous attack from the back. It is a choke, but not the most efficient. You have to react quickly because the fingers can damage your larynx box, and because the assailant, or his buddies, will probably follow with something else, like slamming you in the wall and squeezing.

As soon as grabbed, *lower the chin and lift the shoulders* to ease the pain and loss of oxygen. Start your release maneuver simultaneously; do not give him time to settle the choke.

Usually, such an attack is of the 'pushing-you-forward' type. The best way to deal with it is presented in the coming Illustrations. Go forward with the push to disorient the attacker, do not resist. Then you will start to pivot around the axis of attack while lifting the arm of the pivot side. Just like in the previous section, you lift the arm and pivot *violently* to squeeze his choking hand and damage its joints. Just like in the previous section, *strike down with the elbow* of the raised hand onto the choking arms; use all power possible. This move will also trap his choking arms under your armpit. Poke his eyes with your free hand and kick his groin.

Go with the momentum of the attack and twist with a raised arm for a Downward Elbow Strike on the assailant's arms

DEFENSES AGAINST CHOKES

An alternative way to execute the previous release is presented in the coming Drawings. It is best used in cases *where you have been able to react early*. Just like before, you lift one arm and you pivot violently; but this time the arm is raised bent in chamber position for a Downward Knife-hand Strike. You strike down and diagonally, directly into the side of the opponent's neck. Strike into the *neck* and the *clavicle*. Pull your hand back for an Eye Rake and knee his groin.

A variation of the Release Technique: Strike the attacker's neck instead of his choking arms

Another way to go is to back-kick the assailant, to mollify him before pivoting. In the Illustrations below, you see how to step forward with the push, but while letting your stepping foot come back for a Groin Upward Back Kick. You can then pivot with a lifted arm and take control of the attacker's arm. Strike his arm-locked elbow while pulling the wrist up.

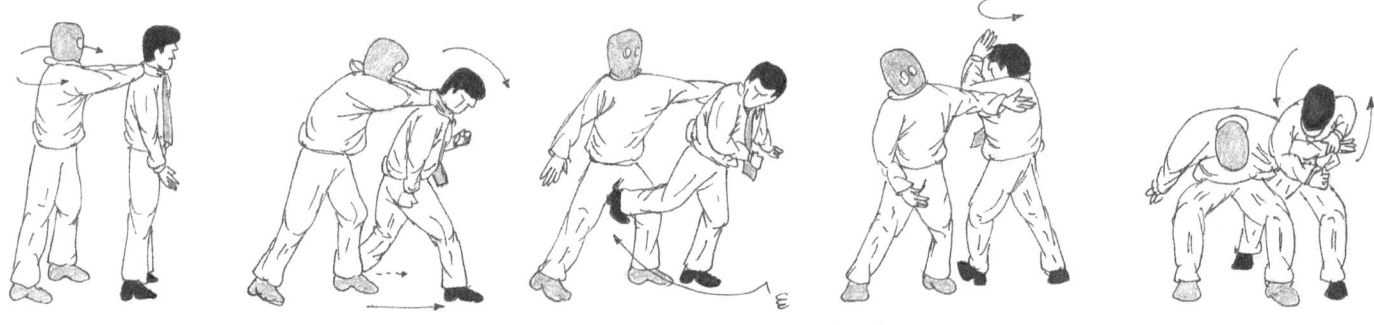

Precede your Release by a Groin Back Kick

In many cases, kicking will be enough to obtain a release. The next Figures, at the top of next page, show how to deliver Back Kicks to the groin, alternating sides, and how to conclude with a Forearm Strike to the side of the neck of the assailant.

➡

KRAV MAGA KICKS

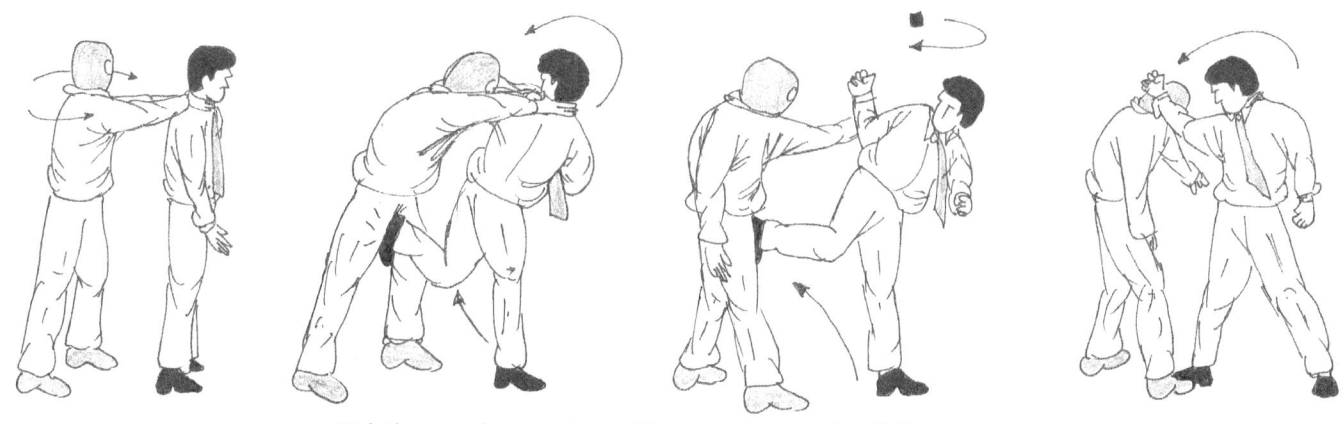

Kick the attacker's groin until he releases you; then follow up

7.3 Rear Naked Choke

The Forearm Choke from behind is an extremely dangerous attack, potentially lethal: you are in mortal danger and are justified in doing everything possible to free yourself.

There are two types of chokes from behind: the **respiratory** choke and the **blood** choke.

The first uses the lower part of the forearm to compress the trachea and restrict oxygen intake. It is painful and can cause physical damage to the larynx box; it can cause death by asphyxiation, but takes longer to act than a Blood Choke.

The *Blood Choke* is less painful, but it can cause irreparable damage and death by restricting the flow of blood to the brain. When done by a trained individual, it is extremely dangerous and fast-acting. It uses the elbow joint as the hinge for both the upper arm and the forearm to press the carotid arteries on the sides of the neck.

Both types are potentially lethal, and you have to react instantly and with no mercy.

Respectively: the Respiratory Rear Choke and the Blood Rear Choke

DEFENSES AGAINST CHOKES

The coming set of Photos illustrates the *general Release Technique* against the Standing Rear Naked Choke. The Photos show a Respiratory Choke, but the general idea is the same for both. Drill the general release before going to the full techniques. You first try to alleviate the pressure on your neck by pulling on the choking arm(s). You then bend and escape rearwards on the attacker's side. Of course, if the Choke is set or close to be, you will certainly need some preceding strike to mellow the attacker.

The classic General Escape Technique against a Rear Naked Choke

This Release Maneuver will hopefully be unnecessary if you can **react before the attacker can even set his Choke**. In the Illustrations below, you can see how to twist at once towards the attacker while headbutting his nose. Follow up with a Groin Knee strike and Rake his eyes for good measure. KISS! Keep it Simple, Stupid...

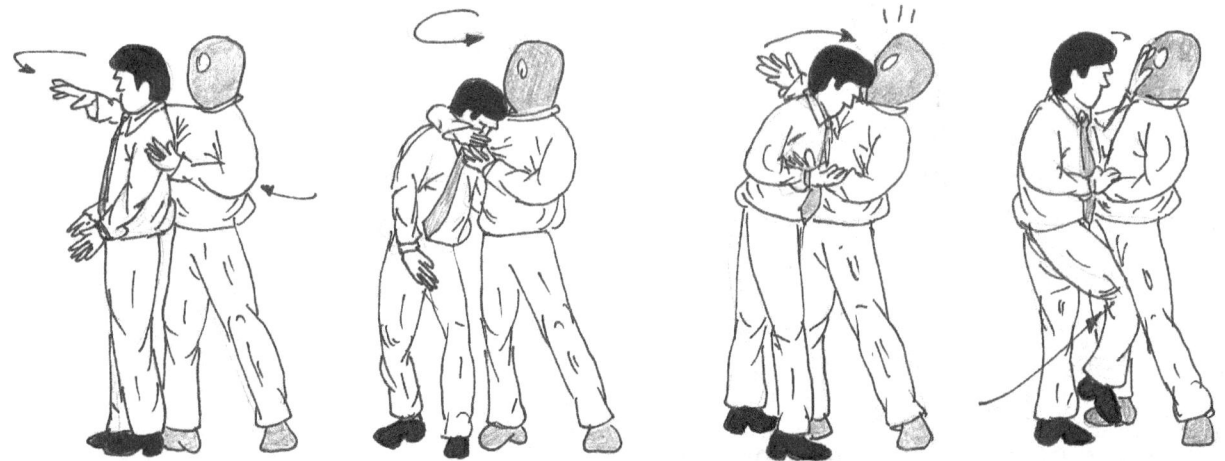

Twist as soon as the attacker extends his arms to set up the Rear Choke; headbutt and kick groin

If you are a little bit too late, with the **Choking hands clasped but no real pressure yet**, proceed as per the next set of Figures. Grab the choking wrist to prevent the pressure and move slightly sideways while bending. Release his wrist to forcefully strike his *groin*. You can now proceed with the classic Release while keeping control of his arm. Lift his twisted arm violently and kick his face (with your knee or shin) as he bends forward. Set your armlock, from where you can keep kicking him or simply pushing him forcefully forward.

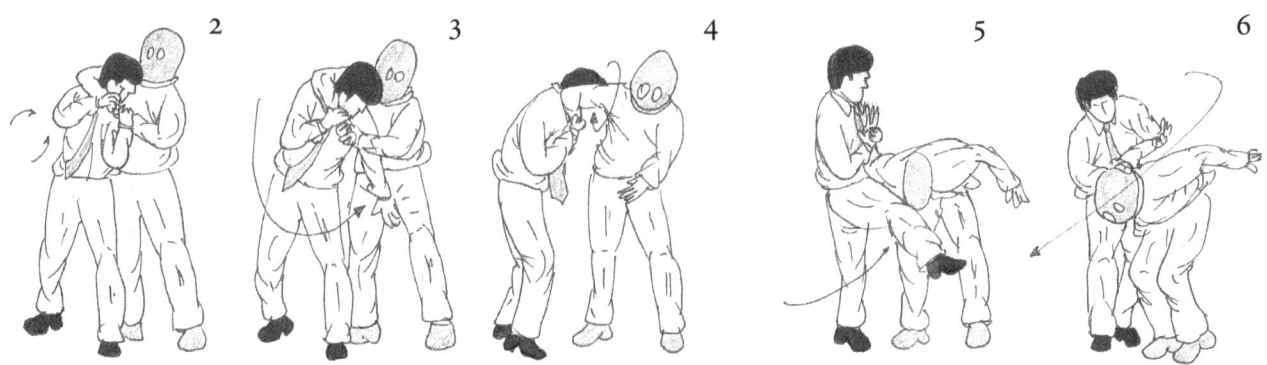

Still early in the Choke set-up, you can easily slap his groin and go into classic release

If you have been surprised and a **Respiratory Choke has been set up**, here is what to do: Throw *immediately* both arms over your head and try to strike his *eyes* with your fingers. Bring then your arms down forcefully while grabbing his choking wrists. You have to make use of the momentum created by having lifted your arms up high (and hopefully reached his eyes). The powerful and sudden pull-down should release the Choke pressure and give you room for the classic Escape/Release. As soon as you are free, pull his twisted arm towards you and kick his groin. Start your own *Retzev*.

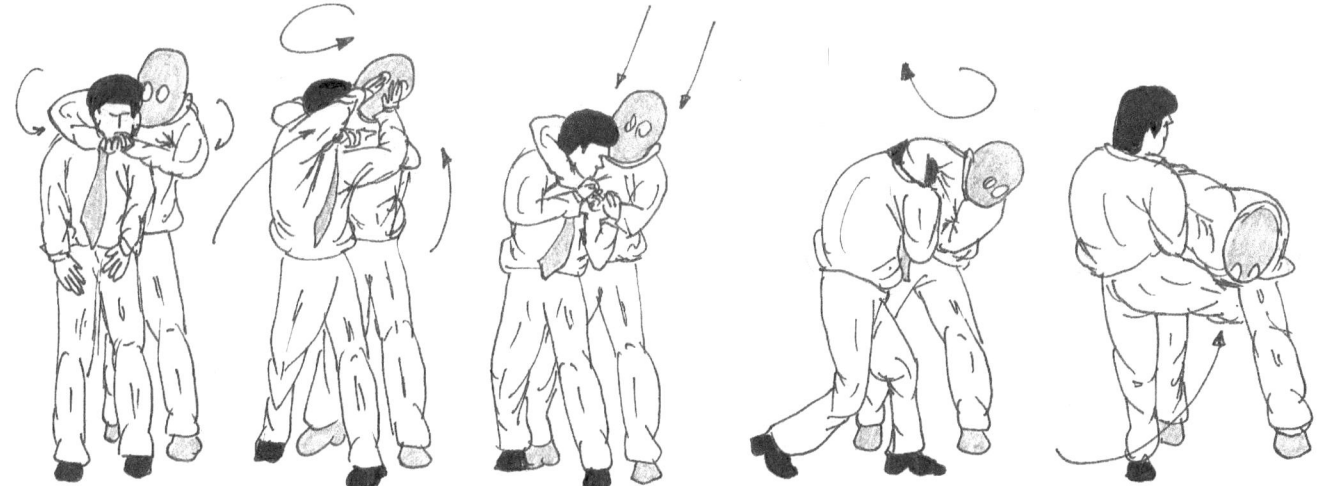

In a Respiratory Choke, attack the eyes to soften his resistance to a classic Release

DEFENSES AGAINST CHOKES

And here is what to do in a **Blood Choke**. We have presented here a more professional Blood Choke, as it will be set by an experienced Martial Artist or a Street Fighter. The throat is caught in a symmetric vise, the choking hand hooks into the elbow joint of the other arm which hand comes behind the head of the victim for additional pressure. This is a very dangerous choke and it shows that the attacker is not a novice.

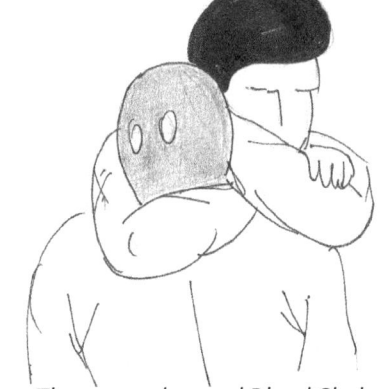

The more advanced Blood Choke

In that case, and in that of a simpler *Blood Choke*, you have to catch the choking arm close to the wrist and *turn your chin towards this 'wrist' side*. Pulling in this way should alleviate the effects of the choke. When grabbing, you should try to **grab a finger** of his choking arm, where it grabs the other arm pushing on your head. Pry *only one finger*, but then bend it back forcefully with breaking it in mind. At the same time, bend your body sideways and make room in front of his groin. Release your hand explosively to elbow or slap his groin (according to the distance). This is life and death, you must strike as powerfully as possible. It is also possible to stomp his foot before this strike in order to draw his attention away. Once his groin has been touched, it is time to go for the classic Escape/Release. As soon as out of the headlock, you should pull his twisted arm towards you and kick his groin. Twist his arm *brusquely* in Arm-lock position and kick his face. You could then break his arm, keep kicking at him or push him (by the twisted arm, in order to damage it). In any case, keep at it; this guy is dangerous.

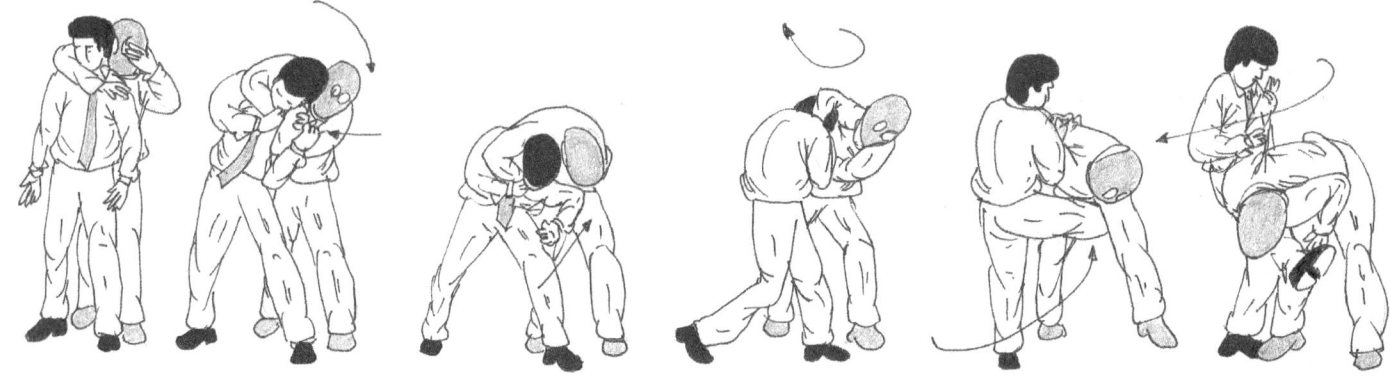

In Blood Choke, bend sideways, twist the chin and grab the wrist to open the vise; then attack the groin

To conclude, we shall present an **alternative Release technique** that should be followed by an *Outer Reap Takedown*. Make a surprising and *explosive pivot* while pulling down on the hold: you get in position to 'break' his posture, with or without placing your leg behind his. It works quite well, but you should be ready to go all the way to the ground with him if he does not fully release you in time. In that case, make sure that you fall heavily on him.

Twist out for a Takedown

The whole technique against a 'professional' Blood Choke; after the Takedown, kick his extended arm to harm his elbow joint and then, stomp his face

Use only that which works, and take it from any place you can find it.
~Bruce Lee

DEFENSES AGAINST CHOKES

8. Defenses against an Armed Assailant

I apologize if the title seems misleading, but this book **will not** present in detail *Krav Maga* defenses against armed attacks. Fighting an armed attacker is not an easy thing, and it belongs to more **Advanced Krav Maga** training. A trainee should first and foremost master the Defenses against an unarmed assailant; he should drill the kicks and other attacks on the heavy bag and he should train as will be detailed in the Afterword. Once he can execute the techniques presented in this book against a not-too-cooperative partner and under stress, the trainee should then proceed to handling an armed aggressor.

The techniques of defense against an armed opponent will be described in a *future book*, already in preparation. This coming work about Advanced Krav Maga will also dwell on tactics and on special techniques.

At this stage, we shall present here a few classic techniques, to whet the reader's appetite and show that the Krav Maga principles stay the same when handling an armed opponent.

8.1 Defenses against a Stick-wielding Assailant

A **stick** is not too-dangerous a weapon. It should not be treated dismissively, but it probably gives the aggressor unwarranted self-confidence.

The principle of handling an opponent holding a stick is to get *as close as possible*, because it negates the advantage of having a stick. Here come a few examples.

The first set of Illustrations shows how you should hop *forward* when confronted by a stick-wielding opponent. In fact, you should try to **preempt** any attack by attacking yourself, as soon as you understand that it is becoming an aggression: the assailant is probably sure of himself and does not expect you to come at him, on the contrary. You can even cower a little before lunging in, so as to strengthen his arrogance, if it is adequate in the specific situation. In the specific example below, you hop forward as soon as you detect that he his lifting his stick to gather momentum. Hop and Roundhouse-kick his *groin*; that will stop him. Then keep kicking until he his fully vanquished.

Preemptive Groin Roundhouse and Low Kick to the knee joint; keep at it...

The principle is always to unexpectedly lunge forward in order to foil the attacker's distance calculations. The next set of Photos illustrates going forward <u>and out</u> against a downward Baseball Bat Strike. You simultaneously go for a Nose Palm Strike (or an Eye Poke). Start you *Retzev* by slapping the groin, stomping the back of the knee or taking him down with an Outer Reap Throw.

Dive low, forward and out to stop him with a Palm Strike

DEFENSES AGAINST AN ARMED ASSAILANT

View from another angle

8.2 Defenses against a Knife-wielding Assailant

Dealing with a **Knife** is a totally different story. Do not fight if you do not have to. If you can flee or if you can hand over your wallet, these are the preferable options. Even *Bruce Lee* used to paraphrase *Demosthenes* and say: "**He who fights and runs away, may live to fight another day.**"

Even the most accomplished Martial Artist or Krav Maga Fighter makes mistakes. Against a Knife attack, the slightest mistake can be lethal: the smallest cut can rattle or incapacitate you and place you at the mercy of a *Coup de Grace*. Forget Hollywood and forget misplaced macho honor. Nothing is worth endangering your life.

But you may have no choice. If fleeing is no option, if your loved ones are in danger, if your gut tells you that handing over your wallet will not save you, then fight with everything you have got and according to the ***aggressive*** principles of *Krav Maga*. Again, it could be beneficial to cower and exaggerate submissive fear before lashing out. **<u>Aggressive preemptive attacks</u>** will generally surprise an armed and over-confident bully.

Here come a few examples.

The coming set of Drawings illustrate how to **lash out at the threatening assailant**, before he starts his own attack. The use of kicks is advised, especially *Body-bent Kicks*. They have longer reach than that the armed hands of the opponent, and bending away gives you some added safety. You should strike vulnerable points and keep kicking <u>without interruption</u>: keep the opponent off-balance and give him no respite that he could use to gather back his wits. In the example, you start with a Body-bent Side kick to his front knee, followed by a rebounding Side kick to his floating ribs. Keep kicking the knee, and, as soon as possible, go for the groin with a Front or a Roundhouse Kick. Do not stop until the assailant is totally vanquished; this is a true case of life-preserving self-defense.

Preempt a Knife attack with a flurry of kicks

It is always about *going forward*. The coming Photos, at the top of next page, show how to evade, forward and in, a low upward Knife Strike to the belly. Control the Knife arm and powerfully Knife-hand-strike it. Follow with another Knife-hand Strike to the side of the neck or the throat, and you can now kick his groin and start destroying him.

DEFENSES AGAINST AN ARMED ASSAILANT

Dealing with an underhand Knife Attack by evading diagonally forward

Going forward does not mean committing suicide. In the next set of Drawings, we see how to deal with a **cutting attack**: evade rearwards, but jump back <u>forward</u> as soon as the blade has passed you. *Forward*. So you will block the hand coming back in the opposite direction. Grab the knife wrist and pull while punching the aggressor's face with the front fist. Switch grabbing hands to claw at his *eyes* with your rear hand; then, kick his *groin*. Twist his wrist and disarm him while pulling him forward. The classic disarm is to hold his wrist firmly while covering his hand with yours, fingers on fingers. You then push his hand towards his wrist to force his fingers to start opening. You immediately 'peel' his fingers out while grabbing the knife handle. Once you have the knife, keep kicking while keeping hold of his wrist.

Evade a slashing strike rearwards, but jump back forward to block the return trajectory

200   KRAV MAGA KICKS

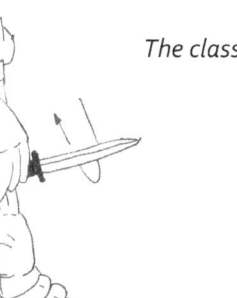

The classic Knife Disarm

In the last example for this section, we will see how to use the aggressor's knife against himself. As illustrated, you go forward on an underhand upward poke to the belly, but you keep your hips back as you block. You wrap the opponent's elbow from above with your other hand and lock the wrist in your blocking elbow, while stepping out. Kick his groin, and once he is so 'mollified', you bend his elbow 'armlock-like'. You can now stab him in the side with the knife he is still holding; just use the power of your hips for the push. You can then push the knife deep in *by kneeing the handle* (not illustrated).

Block an upward low knife stab with a classic downward block and control his arm to force him to stab himself with his weapon

DEFENSES AGAINST AN ARMED ASSAILANT

8.3 Defenses against a Gun-holding Assailant

Everything that was said about the danger of fighting an opponent armed with a knife, is even truer if he holds a *gun*. Do not risk your life for any property: give your wallet and jewelry and do not give it another thought.
But it is sometimes clear that gratuitous violence is the real motive, and your gut could tell you clearly that giving up your stuff will not save you from harm hereafter. In other cases, it can be terrorism or a hate crime on race or other grounds. In the cases you have no choice, *explode* from a cowering attitude (aiming at boosting the confidence of the attacker) to a sudden attack with no mercy.

A real professional criminal will hold you at gun point from a distance. I am sorry to have to say that, in that case, there is not much you can safely do. Try to talk him up and weasel your way closer. Or hope to have something to suddenly throw towards his eyes. But, unlike in Hollywood, your chances are slim.

The better news is that, if hold *<u>at point blank</u>*, your chances are much higher. The only worrying point is that gun deflection can cause stray bullets that can threaten passerby's or even your loved once if they are around. Laymen do not realize that, with minimal training, the deflection of a gun hold close to you is faster than the squeezing of the trigger. This is simply because you initiate the move, and by the time he reacts, you are already out of the firing line. Take a toy gun and try the coming maneuvers with a partner; you'll be surprised how easy it is to deflect before he can fire...

It is still very dangerous though, and the fight should be avoided at all costs if possible. If not...

In the first set of Photos, at the top of next page, you are threatened by a gun held close to you at chest high. Simply clap both hands over the gun *while deflecting it out and moving slightly in*. You then twist the gun violently out and up towards the face of the aggressor. Use the fulcrum method with the trigger as the axis. By doing so, you damage his trigger finger. Pull the gun towards you as he releases it and keep him under the line of fire, but from further away.

Catch and deflect the gun with both hands, break finger and take the gun away

In the next Illustrations, you are threatened with a ***gun touching your back*** (Be sure it is the gun actually touching your back and not his other hand). Twist explosively while sweeping the gun away with your arm; you are simultaneously moving slightly sideways for additional safety. Encircle his armed arm to control it and use the energy of the twist to elbow him in the face. Keep control of the gun wrist while you kick him in the testicles. Go and grab the gun barrel with the other hand, break his trigger finger with a *violent* jerking and pull the released gun out directly into his head.

With a gun touching your back, twist violently to sweep and catch the arm, while also leaning out of the line of fire

DEFENSES AGAINST AN ARMED ASSAILANT

We shall finish this Chapter with the handling of an assailant threatening you with a *long gun*. Stupidly, from close range…

Thanks God, threatening is not shooting yet. You can therefore suddenly *take the initiative*. Hop forward and diagonally out of the line of fire, while grabbing (and deflecting) the gun both at the barrel and around the trigger area. Pull the barrel while elbowing the opponent's face. The Elbow Strike continues in a powerful downward move, enveloping and grabbing the rifle in a full shooter handle. You pull with both hands against his resistance, and suddenly switch directions: push the barrel back and pull on the cross in a fulcrum move around his hands. You can kick him in the groin and complete the pull out of his hands. Take immediately your distance and aim, far enough to avoid any possibility of being disarmed.

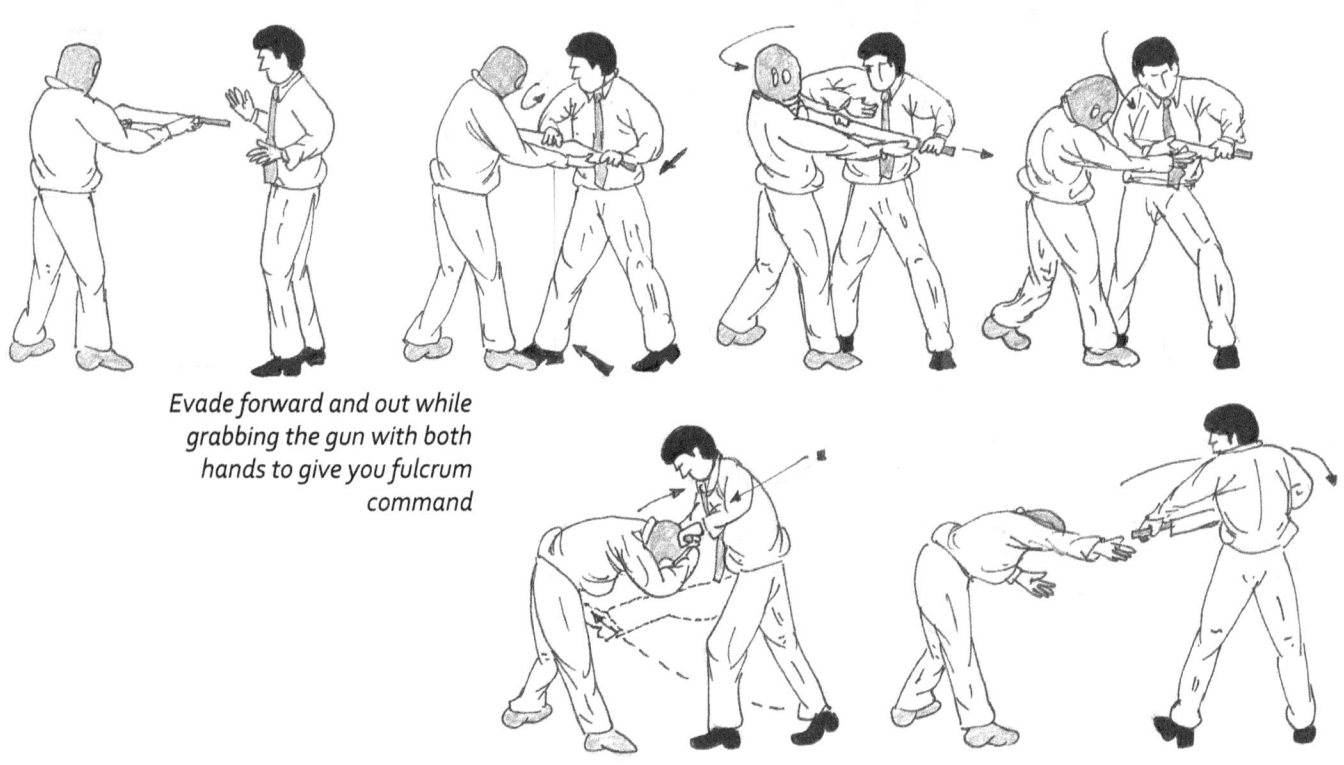

Evade forward and out while grabbing the gun with both hands to give you fulcrum command

Start where you are. Use what you have. Do what you can.
~Arthur Ashe

Afterword

We have come to the end of this presentation of basic *Krav Maga*. Once this book read, you are only at the very beginning of your journey. Here is what should follow.

You should drill the **Kicks** presented in the first part of the book. Perfect the technique and shadow-kick by series of 10, both legs. Once the technique is familiar, you should increase speed while shadow-kicking, and start kicking for power. You should start kicking hanging bags, standing bags, old tires, focus pads and body shields. It is of primary importance to focus on where you are kicking, even when shadow-boxing and in hitting the bag: the knee is not the same height as the thigh, and it is the knee that is the target. The chest is not the floating ribs area. Be conscious of what you are aiming for. You can then start working with a protected partner and start kicking fast, but not at maximum power. Learn to kick somebody who is moving and to concentrate on the specific target.

When you start drilling the **self-defense series**, execute them as presented and slowly. Get familiar with the moves and understand the flow and its probable reasons. Increase speed gradually with familiarity and proficiency. At the beginning, please do follow the *Retzev* moves presented. And drill them many times. In times of stress, like a real-world aggression, it is your body that must take over, intuitively basing itself on the muscular memory. If you have to think about what to do, it means that you have not drilled enough and that you are losing the fight. Drill and drill and drill. When you become proficient, your body will decide by itself which of the Retzev moves are better adapted to the situation and to your affinities. And you are on your way…

Once you have mastered the techniques and their follow-ups, comes the real work. You will need to have your partner 'resist' gradually more to your releases and maneuvers. In real life, your opponent will not stay idle while you react; you have to get used to it. The key word here is: *gradually*. You need a partner with sensitivity: resisting a little bit more, but still let you execute the whole maneuver. Gradually with time, he will make his attacks real attacks, full on, with no 'presents' for you. Thank him, because he is truly helping you. The next steps are as important. Your partner will attack you 'all out' and choosing one specific attack among several possible. You will not know which, so be ready.

The last stage is as important, but really difficult. You'll need another partner or two. While you drill all the exercises presented above, the additional partner(s) will shout at you and push you around while you are defending yourself against the main partner. This additional stress is there to teach you focus and stress management. These training methods are, in fact, the real 'secrets' of *Krav Maga* efficacy. The rest is just KISS (Keep It Simple, Stupid).
Now is time to go and sweat…

And before we say goodbye, here come once more the main basic principles of Krav Maga:

- Attack preemptively or Counterattack as early as possible
- Keep an offensive attitude.
- Target the body's most vulnerable points
- Maximize efficiency for fast neutralization.
- Use offensive defense
- Maintain constant awareness of the battlefield
- Retzev: Keep striking with no interruption until full victory

Si vis pacem, para bellum (If you want peace, prepare for war)
~Latin adage

AFTERWORD

I fear not the man who has practiced 10,000 kicks once, but I fear the man who has practiced one kick 10,000 times.
~ Bruce Lee

And now, dear reader, what is left is for you to start sweating.

Pain is the best instructor, but no one wants to go to his class.
~Choi, Hong Hi, Founder of Taekwon-Do

<u>If you have enjoyed the book and appreciate the effort behind this series, you are invited to write a short and honest review on Amazon.com</u>…It has become extremely difficult to promote one's work in this day and age, and your support would be much appreciated. Thanks!

All questions, comments, additional techniques, special or vintage Photos about Kicks and Krav Maga are welcomed by the author and would be introduced with credit in future editions. Just email:martialartkicks@gmail.com

The author is trying to build a complete series of work that, once finished, could become an encyclopedic base of the whole of the Martial Arts-Kicking realm, a base on which others could build and add their own experiences.
In his endeavors the author has already penned:

- **The Essential Book of Martial Arts Kicks** – *Tuttle Publishing* (2010)
- **Plyo-Flex** - Training for Explosive Martial Arts Kicks (2013)
- **Low Kicks** - Advanced Martial Arts Kicks for Attacking the Lower Gates (2013)
- **Stop Kicks** – Jamming, Obstructing, Stopping, Impaling, Cutting and Preemptive Kicks (2014)
- **Ground Kicks** – Advanced Martial Arts Kicks for groundfighting (2015)
- **Stealth Kicks** - The Forgotten Art of Ghost Kicking (2015)
- **Sacrifice Kicks** - Advanced Martial Arts Kicks for Realistic Airborne Attacks (2016)
-

In the same frame of mind, the following works are in preparation:

- *Combo Kicks*
- *Advanced Krav Maga*
- *Joint Kicks*

Only one who devotes himself to a cause with his whole strength and soul can be a true master. For this reason mastery demands all of a person.
~Albert Einstein

Low Kicks are powerful, fast, and effective exactly what you need to defend yourself in a real life confrontation. And because they are seldom used in sport fighting, they can be a surprising and valuable addition to your free fighting arsenal. While they may seem easy to execute, not all low kicks are simply low versions of the basic kicks. There are specific attributes and principles that make low kicks work. Marc de Bremaeker has collected the most effective low kicking techniques from Martial Arts like *Krav Maga, Karatedo, Capoeira, Wing-Chun Kung-Fu, MMA*, and *Muay Thai*. In this book, he analyzes each kick in depth, explaining the proper execution and outlining applications and variations from self-defense, sport fighting and traditional practice: Hundreds of examples in over one thousand photographs and drawings.

Plyometrics and Flexibility Training for Explosive Martial Arts Kicks and Performance Sports Plyo-Flex is a system of plyometric exercises and intensive flexibility training designed to increase your kicking power, speed, flexibility and skill level. Based on scientific principles, Plyo-Flex exercises will boost your muscles, joints and nervous system interfaces to the next performance level. After only a few weeks of training, you should see a marked improvement in the speed of your kicks and footwork, the power of your kicks, the height of your jumps, your stamina and your overall flexibility. Hundreds of illustrations and photographs will guide you through the basic plyometric and stretching exercises. Once you've mastered the basics, add the kicking-oriented variations to your workout for an extra challenge.

Stop Kicks are among the most effective, sophisticated kicks a fighter can use. And because they hit your opponent at his most vulnerable, they are also the safest way to pre-empt or counter an attack. Stop Kicks are delivered just as your opponent is fully committed to an attack, physically or mentally, meaning it is too late for him to change his mind. Hitting an opponent in mid-attack gives you the added advantage of using his attacking momentum against him. Stop Kicks: Jamming, Obstructing, Stopping, Impaling, Cutting and Preemptive Kicks presents a well organized array of stop-kicking techniques from a wide range of martial arts. Learn Pushing Kicks, Timing Kicks, Cutting Kicks, Obstruction Kicks, and Block Kicks from the hard-hitting styles of Muay Thai, Karatedo, Krav Maga, Tae Kwon Do, MMA and more.

Whether you are on the ground by choice or you have been taken down, whether your opponent is standing or is on the ground with you, whether you are a good grappler or you are trying to keep a good grappler at bay, whether you were caught unawares sitting on the floor or you have evaded down on purpose, whether you are a beginner or an experienced martial artist...this book has the right kick for the situation. In **Ground Kicks**: Advanced Martial Arts Kicks for Ground-fighting from Karate, Krav Maga, MMA, Capoeira, Kung Fu and more, Marc De Bremaeker has created a comprehensive collection of Ground Kicks, with hundreds of applications for sport fighting and self-defense situation. Packed with over 1200 photographs and illustrations, Ground Kicks also includes specific training tips for practicing each kick effectively.

Stealth Kicks will introduce you to the Art of executing Kicks that your opponent will not see coming. This subject has never been treated comprehensively before. Whether you are a beginner or an experienced Artist, you will find suitable Kicks or tips to modify your current techniques to give them stealth. It will help you to score in Sport confrontations or make sure to come on top in real life Self-Defense situations. The *Feint Kicks* presented are based on misdirection: they will aim at provoking a misguided reaction that will open your adversary to the real kick intended. The *Ghost Kicks* presented are based on dissimulation and will travel out of your opponent's range of vision to catch him unawares. Together with general feinting techniques and specific training tips, hundreds of applications will introduce you to the sneaky Art of stealth kicking and will make you a better and unpredictable fighter. Crammed with over 2300 photos and drawings for an easy understanding of the concept of Stealth.

'**Sacrifice Kicks**' will comprehensively present the most important Martial Arts Airborne Kicks: Flying Kicks, Hopping Kicks, Jumping Kicks and Suicide Kicks. They have been dubbed 'Sacrifice' in the spirit of Judo's redoubtable Sutemi Takedowns in which one sacrifices his balance in order to throw his opponent down. *Flying Kicks* are not about showmanship, they are very effective techniques when used judiciously. They need not be necessarily high and spectacular; they can be surprising *Jumping Kicks* and *Hopping Kicks* executed long and low. And *Suicide Kicks* take the Sacrifice principles a little further: they are extremely unexpected techniques delivered airborne, but with little hope of landing on one's feet, unlike classic Flying Kicks. All these realistic maneuvers, coming from Karate, Krav Maga, Kung Fu, TaeKwonDo, MMA, Capoeira, Muay Thai and more, are described with applications and training tips. Over 1000 Photos and Illustrations.

AFTERWORD

OTHER GENRES FROM FONS SAPIENTIAE

AVAILABLE IN PAPERBACK AND KINDLE FORMATS ON AMAZON

The Manual is the definitive guide to Enhanced Concentration, Super Memory, Speed Reading, Note-Taking, Rapid Mental Arithmetic, and the *Ultimate Study Method* (USM).
The techniques presented are the culmination of decades of practical experience combined with the latest scientific research and time-tested practices. The system described herewith will allow the practitioner to:
- Read faster with higher comprehension.
- Remember any type of information instantly.
- Store information in long-term memory.
- Enhance concentration and focus.
- Access deeper levels of the mind.
- Induce relaxation.
- Rapidly perform complex mental arithmetic.
- Master the Ultimate Study Method (USM).

USM is a synergistic combination of established techniques for Concentration, Long-Term Memory, Speed Reading, and Note-Taking. It involves a systematic procedure that allows the practitioner to study any topic fast, efficiently and effectively. USM can be applied to all areas of educational study, academic research, business endeavours, as well as professional life in general.

Rain Fund: A riveting thriller

"…For the safety of the readers, this book ought to come with the disclaimer: leave this book read half-way at your own risk. Unless you are Superman, you won't be able to concentrate on much else until you have read the last page of "Rain Fund". The time has come for Patterson, Ludlum, Dan Brown et al to slide over and make space at the top for Marc Brem." - Shweta Shankar for Readers' Favorite

"…In the good tradition of Ludlum and Grisham. Five Stars" Aldo Levy

"Autistic geniuses charting financial markets; Mobster-fuelled Ponzi schemes; sophisticated hardware viruses; spies; and a rising superpower that strives for dominance – so realistic it is frightening."

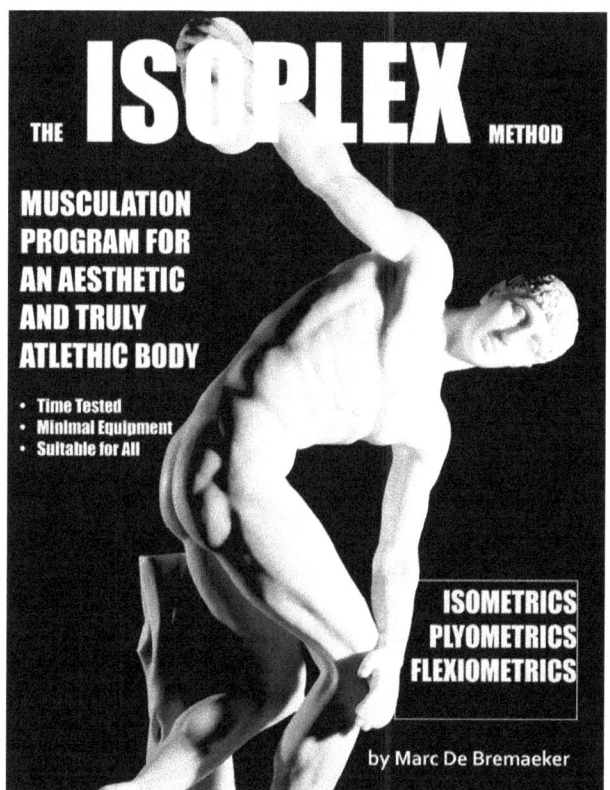

Isoplex stands for Isometrics, Plyometrics and Flexiometrics. The well-organized combination of these three training methods will give the serious trainee the most effective path possible to powerful and aesthetic muscles, in a minimum of time. The method is simply the optimal combination of those three basic tenets of fitness training. It is suitable for men and women. It is suitable for beginners, for athletes of all types, and even for bodybuilders. It is designed to build an aesthetic physique which is also conducive to sport performance and to personal health. ISOPLEX is in fact the modern and more scientific version of the training ideals of Greco-Roman Antiquity. As illustrated by many well-known antique sculptures, the athletes of old had aesthetic bodies based on core musculature and long, well-defined and necessarily efficient muscles. These synergistic training principles are and were universal. They were to be found in ancient Asian Martial Arts and in Body Cultures like Yoga, Chi Kung and many others. A truly athletic and functional body needed for realistic fighting was achieved by a mixture of Isometric exercises, intensive flexibility training and dynamic (Plyometric) drills. Martial Artists and Yogis will immediately grasp the connection. This is the way to train the body for effective and natural aesthetics, and that is what Isoplex concentrates on through an optimal and synergistic time-saving program.

With hundreds of Photos and Drawings and detailing Five complete weekly Programs for all levels.

www.ingramcontent.com/pod-product-compliance
Lightning Source LLC
Chambersburg PA
CBHW080400170426
43193CB00016B/2775